COUNSELLING IN
INDEPENDENT PRACTICE

D1642959

N 0134919 8

· COUNSELLING IN CONTEXT ·

Series editors
Moira Walker and Michael Jacobs
University of Leicester

Counselling takes place in many different contexts: in voluntary and statutory agencies; in individual private practice or in a consortium; at work, in medical settings, in churches and in different areas of education. While there may be much in common in basic counselling methods (despite theoretical differences), each setting gives rise to particular areas of concern, and often requires specialist knowledge, both of the problems likely to be brought, but also of the context in which the client is being seen. Even common counselling issues vary slightly from situation to situation in the way they are applied and understood.

This series examines eleven such areas, and applies a similar scheme to each, first looking at the history of the development of counselling in that particular context; then at the context itself, and how the counsellor fits into it. Central to each volume are chapters on common issues related to the specific setting and questions that may be peculiar to it but could be of interest and value to counsellors working elsewhere. Each book will provide useful information for anyone considering counselling, or the provision of counselling in a particular context. Relationships with others who work in the same setting whether as counsellors, managers or administrators are also examined; and each book concludes with the author's own critique of counselling as it is currently practised in that context.

Current and forthcoming titles

Elsa Bell: *Counselling in Further and Higher Education*
Judith Brearley: *Counselling and Social Work*
Dilys Davies: *Counselling in Psychological Services*
Pat East: *Counselling in Medical Settings*
David Lyall: *Counselling in the Pastoral and Spiritual Context*
Michael Megranahan: *Counselling at Work*
Janet Perry: *Counselling for Women*
Gabrielle Syme: *Counselling in Independent Practice*
Nicholas Tyndall: *Counselling in the Voluntary Sector*
Brian Williams: *Counselling in the Penal System*

COUNSELLING IN INDEPENDENT PRACTICE

Gabrielle Syme

OPEN UNIVERSITY PRESS
Buckingham • Philadelphia

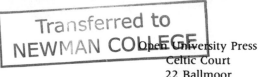

Open University Press
Celtic Court
22 Ballmoor
Buckingham
MK18 1XW

and

1900 Frost Road, Suite 101
Bristol, PA 19007, USA

First published 1994
Reprinted 1997

A catalogue record of this book is available from the British Library

ISBN 0 335 19049 9 (pb) 23079886

Library of Congress Cataloging-in-Publication Data
Syme, Gabrielle, 1943–
Counselling in independent practice / Gabrielle Syme.
    p.   cm. — (Counselling in context)
Includes bibliographical references and index.
ISBN 0–335–19049–9
1. Counselling—History. 2. Counselling—United States—Practice.
3. Counselling—Great Britain—Practice. I. Title. II. Series.
        BF637.C6S9464 1994
            361.3'23—dc20
               93–29252
                 CIP

Typeset by Graphicraft Typesetters Ltd, Hong Kong
Printed in Great Britain by St Edmundsbury Press Ltd,
Bury St Edmunds, Suffolk

To all who have taught me

Contents

Series editors' preface

The rapid increase in the number of counsellors who offer their services in independent or private practice creates for us two immediate causes of concern – the one perhaps contentious, but the other probably universally accepted.

The contentious aspect relates to our deep concern that private practice should be necessary at all. There are undoubtedly those who could convincingly argue for choice in the market place; and clearly there is some justification for encouraging skilled people who cannot find salaried work into the private sector – although it should be added that increased state provision would similarly create employment. Our concern is more with the potential clients or patients. That people should need to pay for help that is often so desperately needed – with problems which generally arise from situations completely beyond their control – raises the same issues as private health care does generally. There is a powerful ethical argument that demands that counselling should respond to need, not to the ability to pay. Given the long waiting lists in many voluntary agencies, there are clearly many in the general population who are unable to afford the mounting bill which private therapy and counselling would demand of them. The National Health Service scarcely touches the surface of this need. It is little wonder that, even in years of economic recession, many counsellors and therapists can earn a living, although they may not always flourish.

We are aware that these are matters over which there is no simple agreement. Left of centre politically though many counsellors purport to be, private or independent practice is clearly here to stay, and it is to her credit that the author of this book shows immense responsibility and care for its delivery. This commands respect and commends the development of dependable practice.

Then there is a second issue around private or independent practice where we imagine a more general consensus exists which provides another cogent reason to underline the message of this volume in the series. The increase in the numbers of counsellors offering a private service has already provided too many examples of inexperienced women and men advertising themselves as practitioners, when in reality they may have little training and experience. In some cases they appear not to have recognized the complexities both of the work they encounter and the organizational aspects and implications of independent practice.

It is these complexities and implications that Gabrielle Syme so clearly and effectively describes. This book demonstrates and reflects the care and responsibility that must be taken by anyone considering independent practice. It is a thoughtful book based upon the experience of a skilled and well trained practitioner who has set her own standards high – a book that invites anyone considering independent practice to follow her model. What is certain is that private independent practice consists of much more than a room with two chairs, and an advertisement in *Yellow Pages*. Gabrielle identifies many issues which opened our own eyes (as experienced practitioners) as we read her book. What we can ourselves be sure of is that no one should even consider offering private counselling and therapy without reading carefully all she has to say.

Moira Walker
Michael Jacobs

Preface and acknowledgements

I have learnt a great deal in writing this book. To my surprise I discovered that 1979, the year in which I first had a private client, coincided with the publication of the first directory of private practitioners by the British Association for Counselling (BAC). I did not realize I was in the vanguard. What I did realize then, and it is still true today, was that there was very little published on the practical side of working in independent or private practice. I had to learn as I went along and inevitably learn from my mistakes. I have been taught by experienced psychotherapists and counsellors, who freely shared their knowledge, by colleagues, by my family, by supervisees, and last but not least by my clients.

Originally this book was entitled *Counselling in Private Practice* and indeed until very recently this was the commonly used name for this sector. However, at recent meetings I have attended, 'independent practice' was being used instead. I have chosen to change the title, because this reflects more accurately both the freedom of the counsellors but also their main problem. It is the independence which is also the greatest problem for clients, because it gives them no safeguards from unscrupulous and unprofessional counsellors. Thus both 'independent' and 'private' will be used and frequently will be interchangeable.

This book will prepare counsellors who are just starting out in independent practice, so that they avoid some of my mistakes, although mistakes they will make. My aim for more experienced counsellors in this sector is to illustrate that there is a body of experience and practice which we have all created. There are

differences in theory and in practice, but there are enough similarities for the profession of 'Chartered Counsellor' not to be a
pipe dream, but near at hand. I hope this book will contribute
to the debate on what is good practice and so raise standards.

It would never have been written without the support of a
number of people. There would have been no book if Moira
Walker and Michael Jacobs had not suggested to me that I had
knowledge to share. I appreciate this and the time they have
given to help me sharpen up my ideas. I have spent considerable
time digging around in the archives of BAC and have been helped
particularly by Judith Baron, Isobel Palmer and Sue Rose. Mary
Swainson gave me a couple of hours of her time and really
made me realize how enthralling the early history was. Archie
Yuill also had a lot to share of the early history. Too many
people to name individually have answered letters to help me
trace the beginnings of counselling in independent practice. Both
Dorothy Heard and Kate Carr shared their knowledge freely
when I first started out in independent practice. Other people
have contributed to my thinking as I have written this book and
made helpful comments about different parts of the manuscript:
in particular Susan Lendrum, Lisa and Peter Green, and Paul
Keeble. My husband, Robert, has had to share me with this
book. His pedantry has made me scream, but his eye for detail
has resulted in many improvements. I am also glad that he
was there. My secretary Brenda Wood has always been in the
background, gently supporting me. I thank them all. While all
this has helped me and added considerable detail to this book,
I take responsibility for all that is written. I hope that I have
done justice to all my mentors and that readers will find, as I
have, that there is always something to learn.

· ONE ·

The development of counselling in independent practice

ORIGINS

Coincidentally both counselling itself and counselling in private or independent practice can be traced back to psychoanalysis as developed by Sigmund Freud in Vienna from about 1890. Freud was medically qualified and set up a private practice in 1886 to support himself and his family. Though originally working as a neurologist, Freud gradually evolved a way of working with hysterical patients which by 1896 he had called psychoanalysis (Jones 1964: 217). Freud's ideas slowly attracted followers who could only learn about these new theories and techniques by attending the 'Psychological Wednesday Society', reading Freud's publications and by being analysed by him. Thus early psychoanalysts such as Alfred Adler, Sandor Ferenczi, Karl Abraham and Otto Rank had a brief apprentice-type training in which they were analysed by Freud. These analysands in turn became analysts, and in this way a cascade effect gradually passed on the knowledge of psychoanalysis. In the process the length of the analysis extended from a brief period, which is much more like a present-day counselling contract, to a very lengthy analysis lasting as long as five years.

This dissemination of psychoanalysis was not restricted to the German-speaking countries. By 1908 Ernest Jones from Great Britain and A. A. Brill from the USA had visited Freud in Vienna, and the following year Freud undertook a lecture tour of North

America. This took the knowledge and practice of psychoanalysis to many countries and resulted in a smaller percentage of analysts actually being analysed by Freud. Predictably, perhaps, one effect was that analysts started changing their practice, rejecting some of Freud's theories and developing their own. Ferenczi, for instance, was concerned to alter psychoanalytic technique to reduce the time taken for an analysis, although he accepted much of Freudian theory, whereas others, such as Adler, Jung, Rank, Stekel and Reich, developed their own theories. Bitterness and mutual recrimination resulted, with a number of these analysts breaking away and developing differing therapies. All these breakaway analysts were private and independent practitioners, as were Freud and Ferenczi.

One major disagreement, which remained an issue within orthodox analytic circles, was whether psychoanalysts should be medically qualified or not. Freud analysed a number of lay people, notably Oskar Pfister, Anna Freud and Otto Rank. He strongly supported lay analysts and wrote a very vigorous defence in 1926 and again in the following year (Freud 1926, 1927). Indeed, he saw psychoanalysis as a totally different profession from medicine or the Church, with its traditional role of hearing confessions and offering absolution, whereas Brill in America insisted that analysts must be medically qualified. This was despite the fact there were already a significant number of lay analysts in practice in the USA who had been analysed and trained in Vienna. Brill was sufficiently influential for the New York legislature to pass a law in 1926 making lay analysis illegal. At much the same time the American Medical Association warned its members not to cooperate with lay analysts (Jones 1964: 584). This prejudice still exists in the USA today with analysts and therapists mostly medically qualified, and professional counsellors required to have a psychology degree. The situation is quite different in Britain, possibly because Freud and his daughter Anna fled to London in 1938. Analysts and therapists are frequently lay people, as are most counsellors, and few counsellors actually have a degree in psychology or training as a clinical psychologist.

It seems likely that this prejudice in the USA against lay people practising as psychoanalysts or psychotherapists led to the introduction of the word 'counselling'. It is claimed that Carl Rogers first used this term in the 1930s to avoid the hostility towards him from psychiatrists, as a lay person and as a psychologist practising psychotherapy (Thorne 1992: 60). He may well have taken the word 'counselling' from pastoral counselling which was already being practised by some ministers.

Nowadays the method of counselling based on Rogers' theories is known as person-centred counselling and belongs to a school known as humanistic. Other examples of humanistic methods of counselling are gestalt and psychodrama. The fundamental attitude that links the different humanistic counselling methods is the view that the client is the greatest expert on him or herself. The actual aim of the counselling is often expressed in terms of the client finding their 'true self' and 'fulfilling their potential'. Brown and Pedder (1979: 179) suggest that the theoretical basis of these three types of humanistic counselling can be traced back to Adler and thence to Freud. Rogers also acknowledged his debt to Rank (Thorne 1992: 9).

Another school of counselling is known as psychodynamic. Being so named, it implies a direct link with the analytic theory and practice of Freud and his followers, as well as breakaway analysts such as Jung and Adler and of more recent theorists and practitioners such as Melanie Klein, Ronald Fairbairn, Donald Winnicott, Harry Guntrip and John Bowlby. While the theories and methods vary, all owe their origins to Freud and acknowledge and work with the unconscious, with the specific aim of enabling the unconscious to become more accessible to consciousness. This happens, for example, as the relationship the client develops with the counsellor in the present recreates and recapitulates many aspects of relationships with significant caregivers from the past. The psychodynamic approach sees the psyche as active and creative, but also as repeating old and familiar patterns. The psyche not only relates to people in the external world but also to different parts of the self in the internal world. In tracing these three main dynamics of the psyche the psychodynamic counsellor has a window into the unconscious and a means of helping the client become more aware of their unconscious behaviour.

The third school of counselling, the behavioural, is much more influenced by psychology and learning theory. The basic belief is that symptoms such as agoraphobia and depression are the result of learning maladaptive habits or irrational beliefs. As these have been learned, then they can in theory be 'unlearned'.

Perhaps the best-known derivative of behavioural counselling in Britain is cognitive behavioural therapy. The suggestion is that depression, for instance, is a result of the way people view the world, distorting and misunderstanding events. The aim of therapy is to discuss each of these negative thoughts and replace them with positive ones.

Two of the three major schools of counselling and many of the types of counselling in each school can trace their origins to Freud and the analysts who broke away from him. The origins of counselling in private practice can similarly be linked back. As we have already seen, Freud and many of his contemporaries originally worked in private or independent practice. At that time medicine, and psychoanalysis as a largely medical discipline, was widely practised privately; to this day this is still true in the USA. This has tended to restrict psychoanalysis to those who can afford it, although by 1935 there were Institutes of Psychoanalysis in Berlin, London, Vienna, Budapest, New York and Chicago offering psychoanalysis free, inevitably to a limited number of people. Such facilities still exist today, extended by the development of counselling in the public sector. This will be examined elsewhere in this series.

Many people hoped that the advent of the National Health Service (NHS) in Great Britain in 1948 would make psycho-analysis or psychotherapy available to the general public. However, for many reasons this did not occur. First, in what was, and still is, a somewhat inhibited society, it was considered to be a self-indulgence to talk about oneself. The few who were psychoanalysed tended to be wealthy and often members of the intelligentsia. As a result, analysis was seen as a luxury for an élite rather than a therapy to meet the specific need of members of the public. Second, though Freud and analysis were well-known, there had been considerable adverse publicity about his views on infant sexuality, which frightened people and brought out hostile reactions. Some of the strongest opposition to analysis came from psychiatrists, the very medical practitioners who could have lobbied for psychoanalysis and psychotherapy within the NHS. A third reason may have been that the fierce disagreements between analysts who remained faithful to Freud and the others who broke away, understandably made outsiders suspicious. Last but not least, there was little actual proof that psychoanalysis or psychotherapy cured specific mental illness. It was unlikely that public funds would be spent on something until it was proved to be effective, even though many individuals attested to its success. This then questions the methods of collecting evidence.

However, with the belief that there was no proof of effectiveness, the view was: 'Leave psychoanalysis to those who are prepared to pay.' To this day psychoanalysis and psychotherapy are not readily available from the NHS. For example, in a city as large as Leeds the first psychotherapy department was established in the main teaching hospital in 1979 with one full-time consultant. At the time of writing there are two full-time consultants and two senior registrars for a population of about 706,000. This results in long waiting-lists, and in some places only time-limited therapy being available, which is not suitable for all patients. This lack of provision is partly related to the power of psychiatry. There is little evidence that its methods offer a cure to emotional disturbances, but it is an established, and often very conservative profession, with a powerful lobby, which is resistant to other approaches to helping people find emotional well-being. Counselling is similarly affected by the power and attitude of psychiatrists. The combination of the conservatism of the population at large with its fear of self-indulgence, and the lack of support from psychiatrists, may be responsible for the grossly inadequate provision of counselling within the NHS. Yet many people are seeking counselling and believe it to be effective. With such a low level of provision, the majority of people have had to turn to the voluntary or independent sector or to a counselling service.

Up to this point I have referred to psychotherapy and counselling as two distinct terms. It is common in the USA for the two terms to be used interchangeably, and person-centred practitioners see no difference. However, this is not as true in Britain where, while a considerable overlap would be acknowledged, differences are also recognized. In general, counselling tends to be for a short time (less than 20 sessions) and focuses on a particular crisis, whereas psychotherapy continues for longer and deals with more deep-seated personal issues. Having said this, some psychotherapists such as Ryle (cognitive analytic therapy) and Mann (time-limited therapy) offer short-term contracts and some counsellors offer long-term exploration (Einzig 1989: 8). There are no neat divisions, and this difficulty has been identified in some of the research sponsored by the National Council for Vocational Qualifications, and by the Advice, Guidance and Counselling Lead Body. These two bodies are responsible for establishing National Standards and appropriate ways of accrediting and awarding qualifications. Considerable time and money has been spent to establish the similarities and differences in the competencies necessary in the four professional areas of psychology (counselling, occupational, clinical and educational), counselling and psychotherapy. Few differences have been found.

It is my intention that this book should address both counsellors and psychotherapists in independent practice. Therefore, although I predominately use the words counselling and counsellor, much of what I write is also valid for psychotherapy and the psychotherapist. This is particularly so where as a psychodynamic counsellor I consider the different ways in which counselling in independent practice can be set up to enhance or inhibit the understanding and exploration of the unconscious. I do not, however, confine my observations about independent practice to the psychodynamic school, recognizing that the other main approaches outlined are equally well-represented in the independent sector.

GROWTH

Counselling as a planned and organized activity started in Britain in the late 1940s. Initially, training in counselling was mainly available to volunteers of the National Marriage Guidance Council (NMGC) (see Tyndall 1993), to some youth workers and to some priests (see Lyall, forthcoming). By the late 1950s several counselling courses had been set up in universities. These were specifically for teachers, as part of in-service training.

The movement of counselling from the voluntary or public sectors into the private, independent sector seems to have been very gradual. My working definition of 'working in private practice' involves accepting private referrals, counselling clients in one's own time, using one's own premises and charging a fee. The actual number of clients that such self-employed counsellors see may vary from one or two a week to a full case-load of 20–30 clients per week.

Although there had been small numbers of both psychoanalysts and psychotherapists working in Britain in the independent

sector both pre- and post- the Second World War, there appears
to have been no one specifically calling him or herself a counsellor in the private sector until the late 1950s. In 1956 there
was at least one counsellor working privately in his own time
and using his own premises, but charging no fee. The first person I know to have counselled privately and charged a fee did
so in 1960. Throughout the 1960s interest in counselling was
growing and each year a few more people started working independently. This interest resulted in a pressure group forming a
steering body in 1970. This group called itself the Standing
Conference for the Advancement of Counselling (SCAC). Its aims
were to draw together counsellors from a variety of settings and
to interest the government and educationalists in counselling.
They were perhaps unaware of individuals in private practice,
for all the original members represented organizations. It was
not until 1972 that the committee decided to allow individual
members to join SCAC. This standing conference met regularly
until 1977, when it disbanded with the formation of the British
Association for Counselling (BAC). BAC incorporated individual
members from the outset, as well as organizational members.
This reflected the changing reality, as throughout the 1970s the
number of counsellors in private practice grew. By 1979, when
BAC produced their first referral directory, 127 people registered
as independent, private practitioners.

It is relevant at this point to introduce a caveat on these
numbers. No survey has been conducted to find the number of
counsellors in Britain, let alone those in independent practice.
The only figures that are freely available come from the number
of entries in the directories published by BAC. These directories
were originally published specifically to enable members of BAC
to refer their clients, who were moving, to another counsellor
in private practice. The first three directories were simply called
referral directories (1979/1980, 1981/1982, 1983). The fourth
was called a *Counselling Resources Directory* (1985) and the last five
have all been entitled *Counselling and Psychotherapy Resources
Directory* (CPRD) (1988, 1989, 1990, 1991/1992, 1993). Regardless
of title, all nine contain entries from people defining themselves
as counsellors, as psychotherapists and as psychoanalysts, or in
two of these categories. Obviously this leads to an overestimate
of the number of counsellors. It also appears that some counsellors in the directories have never taken private referrals but included their name 'just in case they ever need to work privately',

whereas others were included more than once because they worked in more than one place.

All the directories have another in-built bias that leads to an overestimate of numbers. Anyone who is a member of BAC, or a member of the Institute of Psychosexual Medicine, or a qualified practitioner of a member organization of the United Kingdom Standing Conference for Psychotherapy (UKSCP) can have their name included in directories or registers. Obviously a directory that allows entrants to make their own definition of being a counsellor or psychotherapist is likely to have a high number of entries; the more so where no fee is charged for having one's name included. A fee was introduced for the BAC 1991/1992 directory, but it was only applicable to people who had been in the 1990 directory (i.e. new entries were free – a somewhat idiosyncratic stipulation). Despite this, or perhaps because of this, the number of entries has continued to increase. This obviously raises the question of whom can actually be called a counsellor, and who decides this. As yet there is no agreement in the UK, although efforts are being made to resolve this (see Chapter 6).

Although it is arguable that these figures are overestimates, the converse may be true: they may be underestimates. The first referral directory from BAC only listed counsellors who were members, although at that time there were specialist counsellors such as sex and marital counsellors already practising in the independent sector, who were not members of BAC (many were members of the Association of Sex and Marital Therapists). Furthermore, not all counsellors in the independent sector choose to pay for their name to be included in these directories. Some choose to be on the register of their own training body, profession or society; for instance, they are included on registers of the Institute of Psychosynthesis or of the Gestalt Psychotherapy Training Institute or of the British Psychological Society. Nevertheless, the numbers from the different directories published by BAC, while inaccurate, can be used to demonstrate trends.

These numbers (Figure 1.1) show a substantial growth in counselling in the private sector since 1979/1980. Over the ten years from 1980 the number of individual entries has increased ten-fold from 127 to 1,270. In the following year there was a further increase to 1,764 entries (1991/1992); followed by a smaller increase to 1,924 in the most recent directory (1993). Of

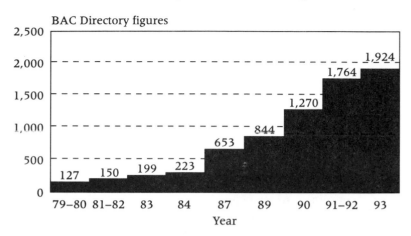

Figure 1.1   Number of Counsellors in BAC Directory 1979–1993

course, these dramatic increases could simply be the result of better publicity and a wider circulation of application forms for inclusion in the CPRD. However, I do not believe this is sufficient explanation or one that accurately reflects the real situation.

The increase in counsellors in independent, private practice follows a more general trend of increasing numbers of people employed professionally in a new social function involving 'personal helping' (Halmos 1978: 31). The professionals identified by Halmos, initially in 1965 and in a second edition of his book *The Faith of the Counsellors* in 1978, were psychiatrists, psychoanalysts (lay or medically trained), psychologists, social workers and counsellors. Between 1960 and 1976, Halmos found an almost four-fold increase in members of these professions from 5,650 to 21,350. This latter figure includes 800 counsellors, whereas none were included in the 1960 figure. At the time of the formation of BAC in 1977 there were 1,400 individual members. Some of these were practising counsellors working in a variety of settings (employed by organizations such as schools, colleges and universities, as well as others working for voluntary agencies and in private practice); others were trainers of counsellors and there were also some students in training. The overall membership of BAC increased almost four-fold from 1,858 in 1979/1980 to 7,218 in 1990/1991. Comparing this with the ten-fold increase in counsellors in the independent sector over the same period, clearly there has been a much steeper rise in the number of counsellors in this sector than in the number of counsellors in general.

In looking for explanations for this increase in independent, private practice, I can only offer speculation rather than hard evidence. There may well have been different factors at work in the 1970s when counsellors first moved into private practice than in the surge in the 1980s. This is partly because the background was so different between the two decades.

In the early 1970s there was an established voluntary sector, a small number of counsellors employed in schools and institutes of further and higher education and almost no private work. With counselling well-established in the voluntary sector, the ethos included considerable resistance to the professionalization of counselling. This lobby was so vehement that professional counselling, particularly in private practice, was strongly disapproved of by many counsellors. The introduction of a number of full-time courses, particularly for teachers, led to an increase in people who described themselves as professional counsellors and who indeed were paid for their work. This may have started to turn the tide of opinion, since it became more acceptable to be paid for this type of work. It is interesting that some voluntary organizations now pay some of their counsellors (e.g. RELATE).

During the 1970s counsellors from the USA had a profound influence on counselling in the UK. A number of the early full-time courses were staffed by Americans or by people who had gone to the USA to be trained. Halmos (1978: 47) gives a figure of 50,500 for professional counsellors in the USA. The difference between 800 in the UK and 50,500 in the USA cannot be accounted for simply by differences in population. Professional counselling was already established in the USA and acted both as a source of training and a model, particularly for independent practice. This continued to be true throughout the 1970s and 1980s.

Another feature of the 1970s was the setting up of counselling services in universities and polytechnics and the appointment of professionally trained counsellors. This did not occur in schools where staff cut-backs hit school counsellors. As a result, a number of teachers, who had originally trained as counsellors, were not employed solely for pastoral work. Many were both disappointed and frustrated at not being able to use their training; some left to find employment as counsellors elsewhere, while others moved into the private sector.

A similar exodus of professionals occurred in social work in the early 1970s. As a result of the Seebohm Report (1968) the profession changed course from specialist professional associations such as child-care workers, psychiatric social workers and hos- pital social workers to a generic model of social-work practice. Some of the social workers, especially those involved in coun- selling specific client groups, looked for ways of continuing this work. Some could only achieve this by changing career. Some chose counselling, particularly part-time and privately, to resolve their dilemma.

A frequent answer from counsellors asked about their deci- sion in the 1970s to work privately (whether or not they charged a fee), is that they received many requests for counselling. A number of marriage-guidance counsellors, for example, were asked to offer counselling on non-marriage issues. Similarly, priests found they were asked for counselling by non-parishioners. This indicates that there was a steadily increasing group of people who had heard of counselling and its success. Indeed, certain key figures in the counselling world, for instance, Hans Hoxter, the founder of the International Round Table for the Advance- ment of Counselling (IRTAC), saw the 'education' of the public and of government as one of their prime tasks.

By the beginning of the 1980s there was a small but growing body of trained counsellors, working either part-time or full- time in the independent sector, and a small but growing number of people aware of counselling as a potential source of help in a crisis. Thus the potential for a rapid increase in private work existed in the 1980s, in sharp contrast to the early 1970s. There are further differences in the background of the 1970s and 1980s. By the early 1980s there were a few counsellors employed by large companies, most institutes of higher education employed at least one counsellor and there was an even stronger volun- tary sector.

Throughout the 1980s awareness of the value and existence of counselling continued. An attitudinal change was also evident, so that clients were less likely to be labelled as 'weak' or 'going mad'. This change in attitude is also reflected in the media, so by the end of the decade 'soaps' such as *The Archers* on the radio, and *Brookside* and *EastEnders* on television, had storylines in which characters turned to counsellors for help. This is positive public- ity and inevitably leads to more people seeking counselling.

Additionally, many more counselling courses have been established, resulting in a greater number of people describing themselves as counsellors. However, this increase in qualified counsellors in the 1980s has not been matched by an increased availability of paid counselling jobs. As a result, there are more counsellors than paid jobs, which in turn has meant more people setting up in the independent sector. It should be said at this point that there is little quality control of courses or counsellors, so the increased numbers of counsellors does not necessarily mean higher standards. This raises the issue of what training and qualifications a counsellor should have to set up in private practice. This and other related issues will be discussed in later chapters.

The awareness of counselling and the need for trained counsellors has come not only from education but from a greater recognition of need. In the 1980s there was a significant increase in self-help groups such as the British Association of Cancer United Patients (BACUP), the Miscarriage Association, the Carers' National Association, the Stillbirth and Perinatal Death Association (SANDS) and many others. In each case a group of people in a similar situation met and offered each other support. They found that provision had to be made for some of the group who needed professional support and counselling. Some groups would pay for this, others would negotiate voluntary, unpaid support. This could lead to the professional counsellors being asked to give some one-to-one help, and also being asked to train members of the self-help group in counselling. Yet again, this resulted in an increasing pool of people who considered themselves 'trained counsellors'. A proportion of them have subsequently wanted remuneration for their skills and so sought jobs or moved into independent practice. At the same time, the more that voluntary groups have recognized the need for counselling, the more work has become available to counsellors in the independent sector.

The recognition of self-worth is frequently one of the stated aims of personal counselling or counselling training. Some agencies have become particularly vulnerable to the success of their training through losing well-trained volunteers or workers to the independent sector. Particular examples are the National Marriage Guidance Council/RELATE and Westminster Pastoral Foundation (WPF), who both have counsellor-training courses of a high quality. A significant number of student counsellors and counsellors in the independent sector were first trained through these two organizations. Their reason for leaving the agencies was that they had come to value themselves, their training and their counselling skills, and they wanted remuneration which also recognized this. The only way to achieve it was to leave the voluntary sector. Many of these have been women in mid-life who became voluntary counsellors while they had young families, but then looked for a new career once their family commitments lessened. Counselling in the independent sector was a particularly attractive possibility in the later 1980s when the general job market contracted. Instead of (often unsuccessfully) seeking employment, they could be self-employed, setting their own working pattern and environment, the number of hours and their income. The result of this, and of society's bias towards women being 'the carers', has been that 75 per cent of counsellors in the 1993 CPRD are women.

Apart from a personal drive to seek remuneration as a counsellor, the political force of 'Thatcherism' also encouraged this move. At the same time it probably increased the number of people seeking counselling. I have no hard evidence to support this latter statement: it is based on the increased number of enquiries BAC received from people asking for names of counsellors and the impression of myself and other counsellors. Two facets of this political change may be relevant in considering the increase in numbers of counsellors in independent practice. First, the 'cult of the individual' meant that people were encouraged to create small businesses: this of course included counsellors. Second, the drive to make the NHS (and educational establishments) financially accountable for their activities has resulted either in no expansion or in an actual cut-back of services, that cannot prove themselves to be cost-effective. This whole ethos, in addition to the difficulty of proving therapeutic efficacy, has slowed the expansion of counselling posts and also resulted in disaffected counsellors leaving employment because of a lack of career opportunities. Once again, the shortfall between trained counsellors and paid posts has resulted in private work becoming one viable option.

There may have been fewer paid posts for counsellors but there has been no shortage of people seeking counselling. This may have been partly another offshoot of 'Thatcherism'; for both strong individualism and the rapid changes in society and the public sector have been very stressful for many people. A significant number have sought help from counsellors for stress management. Another reason is that there has been a wider acknowledgement of problems. This has enabled many people to seek counselling in recent years, who previously would not have done so. This increased demand has frequently led to long waiting-lists in work-based or other counselling services, so an independent counsellor has been sought. Indeed, for some the fear of disapproval from their employers has meant that such a counsellor was preferable from the start. This choice has been reinforced by the encouragement of the individual to buy their own help. This increase in demand for private counselling has resulted, in turn, in increased numbers of counsellors joining the independent sector. This is probably because both volunteer and employed counsellors have found themselves asked more and more frequently if they themselves can either see someone privately or else recommend someone in the independent sector. A proportion of them have responded to this pressure and joined the independent sector themselves either part-time or full-time.

A further factor that has resulted in increased demand for counselling during the 1980s has been a significant change in attitude of many people to their own health. Some have become interested in a holistic approach to medicine. This has led them to question whether illness has an organic cause *per se*, or whether the causes are a much more complex interplay between emotional and physical well-being. The result has been more people seeking an understanding and acceptance of their emotions; for some, counselling has been a route to this self-knowledge.

There has also been some disillusionment either with the efficacy or the dependency effects of drugs for depression and anxiety. This has led people to seek an alternative to medication. When psychotropic and anxiolytic medicines became widely prescribed in the 1960s, they were heralded as wonder drugs without any addictive properties. Gradually this has been proved to be untrue, particularly in the case of valium and librium. Scepticism was further fuelled by drugs such as thalidomide which caused severe developmental abnormalities. The effect of this for some people has been the rejection of drug therapy for depression and anxiety, and a search for alternative routes of help. Again, counselling is one choice, as can be concluded from a recent survey by the Royal College of Psychiatrists. They found that 85 per cent of 2,000 respondents believe that depression was caused by life events and that counselling rather than medication would be the most helpful intervention.

Such social pressure has led some General Practitioners (GPs) to employ counsellors, but demand has exceeded supply (see East, forthcoming). Here again the effect seems to have been to convince some counsellors that they can respond to this demand by moving into the independent sector and creating a viable career for themselves.

The actual distribution of counsellors in the independent sector is very uneven. Using the 1993 BAC CPRD there were, as would be expected, many more counsellors in London and the neighbouring counties. Thus in London 608 counsellors registered, in Middlesex 63, in Surrey 150, in Sussex 72, in Kent 66, and in Essex 59. These numbers contrast with Northern Ireland where only 3 counsellors were registered, and with Derbyshire and Cumbria where respectively there were 8 and 4 counsellors registered. Wherever large cities are in an area there tend to be more registered counsellors. For instance the number in Greater Manchester was 37, in the West Midlands (including Birmingham) was 36 and in West Yorkshire (including Leeds and Bradford) was 40. However, this was not a consistent pattern, for Merseyside (including Liverpool) had only 21 registered, and South Yorkshire (including Sheffield) had only 15. This uneven distribution can only be partly explained by the differences in population and the number of training courses in an area.

For a variety of reasons, counselling in independent practice has become an attractive career, although it is not without its dilemmas for many counsellors, nor without its problems for those who wish to safeguard the standards of counselling. There is an ever-present danger of standards being eroded in some areas of Britain where demand exceeds supply, either because there are two few counsellors, for instance Northern Ireland, or because there is too much demand for the counsellor provision, as in West Yorkshire. This imbalance could result in inadequately trained and insufficiently skilled counsellors being attracted to private practice. This is particularly dangerous for a profession which is self-regulatory (see Chapter 6). A bad press could cause a collapse in demand. This in turn could reduce the amount of work available just as much as too many counsellors in the independent sector.

Having traced the historical origins of counselling and private practice and its growth in the last 20 years, the next chapter looks at the setting of counselling in independent practice in present-day society. Specific questions are addressed, such as: what are the forces that drive people to seek private counselling? What are the effects of not working in an institutional setting? What difference does it make when the client is the employer? What are suitable premises for counselling? How does a counsellor in private practice find clients?

· TWO ·

Counselling in independent practice

WHY INDEPENDENT PRACTICE?

A principal factor in the development of counselling in independent or private practice, as I showed in the last chapter, is demand. But 'why the demand?' At a simplistic level, demand is created because the individual requests for counselling outstrip supply, whether on the NHS, through occupational health provision or welfare services supplied by employers, or from voluntary agencies and counselling services. Behind this phenomenon are much more fundamental questions of relevance to all counsellors:

What changes in society have occurred to result in the need for people to seek help from counsellors?
What happened before there were counsellors?
Are there even more people in need of counselling?
Should there be provision of counselling paid for out of taxes in the same way as the NHS, so that it is available to anyone who asks?

The first two questions are interrelated and have been extensively addressed by Halmos (1978) in discussing 'the coming of the counsellors'. In summary he suggests that 'scepticism about the effectiveness of political solutions' inevitably results in a 'personalist' phase. In this phase there has been a proliferation of professional workers who believe that only by offering 'personal access to the single individual seeking help' can any 'marked and lasting difference' be made. He suggests, among other reasons, that this new profession of counsellors could only emerge because of the decline in religious practice.

Clergy, of course, were not the only 'listeners' concerned with individuals in the past. GPs also fulfilled this role, as well as 'wise people' in tight-knit communities and in families. Modern mobility has destroyed these communities and networks, and changed families from extended, but close family structures, to the basic nuclear family. Medical advances have changed the style of working of many GPs and also the expectations of their patients. In the first 40 years of this century there were few drugs to treat disease. Doctors therefore often acted in a supportive role to the family while the patient either survived or died. Modern drugs have changed the situation dramatically, with many common diseases cured by a course of medication. This has changed the GP, at worst, into a dispenser of prescriptions with some patients expecting a drug for any physical ill. In addition, patients are frequently referred to hospital when terminally ill, so GPs are not expected to give emotional support. These changes have left patients with less expectation of being able to talk to or of being 'listened to' by the doctor. Yet recent surveys have shown that as many as 30 per cent of all GPs' patients have been found to be suffering from emotional distress without organic disease, suggesting that emotional support is what they actually need.

With people no longer turning to clergy and doctors, and networks of care in families and communities being less available, there is a void. This has been filled by professional counsellors (in Halmos' sense), with the actual profession of counselling growing, driven by the many factors outlined in the first chapter. Currently demand exceeds supply, which suggests that counselling is a form of help for which there is a perceived need, but inadequate provision. This raises the question of whether the government should fund counselling as a service for all, paid for through taxation, in the same way as health care and education. Were there sufficient publicly funded counselling, then choosing a private practitioner would become an active choice, rather than a choice driven by lack of provision and only being possible if a person can afford it. These are very negative reasons for choosing a counsellor in the independent sector.

In a mixed economy, where choice between a public and a private service exists, there are positive reasons behind the deliberate choice. For instance, autonomy involves the freedom to choose whether to pay for the help or not. With adequate counselling provision, a client can meet several counsellors before deciding which person and method of working to choose. At present there is little choice. It could well be that all that is available is the counsellor provided by a GP (perhaps offering six sessions), an employer or a voluntary agency. There may also be only one person in private practice in the area, but at least this person may offer a service better matched to the client's needs in terms of number of sessions, frequency of sessions and personal convenience.

Reasons for choosing counselling in the independent sector might not always be good ones, although they may be valid. A client may fear disapproval from her or his employer, making an employee seek a counsellor in the independent sector rather than using an in-house service. Such fears may be based in reality or be fantasy. If the latter, then this becomes part of the counselling work. So would the acknowledgement by a client that shame at needing help had led them to choose the independent sector, in the belief that it is easier to keep the counselling secret. Another reason that needs questioning is the idea that the service is up-market or better because it is paid for. A further example is the belief that *no* service is good unless paid for; indeed, that the best counsellors are in the private sector. Needless to say, there is no evidence to support such a belief.

WHO IS THE EMPLOYER?

In the private sector the most common employer is the client. This has its difficulties for both the counsellor and the client, since there is no institutional buffer. The result is that the client lacks the safety of the knowledge that an institution or agency has chosen the counsellor, presumably from a range of applicants, and that he or she is considered to be competent. Without this safety net the client needs to ascertain specific facts about the counsellor, such as qualifications, accreditation, supervision, code of ethics and of practice, etc. This will be dealt with in more detail in Chapters 3 and 4.

Neither do clients in independent practice have a clear route for complaint as they would seeing a counsellor in an institution or agency. The client has no obvious consumer rights since it is possible that a counsellor does not belong to a professional association that demands acceptance of a code of ethics and of practice as a prerequisite for membership. This is a reason for the necessity of a client to establish that certain criteria are met before choosing a particular counsellor (see Chapter 4).

It is also difficult for the counsellor who lacks an institutional buffer. A counsellor in private practice has to carry the total responsibility for the way he or she works, for a code of ethics, for the hours worked, the clients chosen, the length of counselling sessions and the counselling work, and the fees charged. If private practice seems a luxury, it is not without its own pressures.

Another issue associated with the lack of institutional support is that absence through holidays, but more especially through illness, means having to make arrangements for emergency help and cover, particularly for very vulnerable clients. When there is an institution, clients often develop a transference relationship with it, quite apart from one with the counsellor/therapist. While at times this can complicate the counselling unless recognized and worked with, it can be an advantage when a counsellor is ill or on holiday. Indeed, therapists at the Maudesley are said to call the institute the 'brick mother', because the transference of patients to the institution as a whole seems to prevent the expected disturbances in therapy as a result of the registrars moving every six months (Temperley 1984).

Further consequences of being self-employed are that there may be little income when the counsellor is ill; the counsellor has to arrange personal insurance to cover both total loss of earnings through permanent disability and for professional indemnity; and the counsellor has to consider buying a personal pension. These issues will also be looked at in more detail in Chapter 4.

A recent development has resulted in another type of work for counsellors in the independent sector. This is the formation of organizations who offer major companies the service of an Employee Assistance Programme (EAP). Most EAPs make a contract with a company and then employ counsellors in the private sector to undertake the counselling. The particular issues related to this work will be discussed in Chapter 5, as will other instances where the client is not directly employing the counsellor or where it is unclear who the employer actually is.

WHERE TO COUNSEL?

In considering a choice of premises, there is the related question of working alone or in a group or team. Some counsellors in the independent sector form a group practice with other counsellors. In these practices, several counsellors work from the same premises, each having their own room if they work full-time; alternatively, if they work part-time, they may share rooms. In some of these group practices each member works in isolation; in others, counsellors work as part of a team, with clients being assessed and then allocated to the most suitable counsellor. An alternative is to form a group practice with practitioners of various branches of alternative medicine. One example is the grouping together of a counsellor, an acupuncturist, a reflexologist and an aromatherapist.

The advantages of group practice are obvious: the members of the group share the running costs of premises, receptionist/ secretary and telephone. There is also the security of knowing that there are other people working in the building. There are even greater advantages for a group practice of counsellors because there is the mutual support of co-workers with the same problems and concerns, who share an understanding of the need to manage office procedures in ways that help the counsellor–client relationship. A group of counsellors also offer each other the possibility of peer supervision and cover for vulnerable clients when a counsellor is on holiday or ill.

It is likely that a group practice would need a receptionist and would be able to afford to employ one. Should they do so, the receptionist would need training to manage some of the problems that arise for counsellors and clients when a group of counsellors work together. These centre around the client having a relationship with their own counsellor and with the receptionist but also with other counsellors in the group and with the group practice, although these latter two relationships may be more imagined than real. Clients may try to play one member of the group off against another by, for instance, telling the receptionist that they want to change counsellor, or they can use a receptionist as an intermediary when cancelling sessions, or making a sudden ending. A receptionist could also be the only person to know that someone has cancelled their initial assessment session several times. In all these instances a receptionist needs training that explains what the counsellors need to know. Role-play assists in learning how to manage these interactions in such a way that the client is helped, the receptionist becomes clear about his or her role, the importance of the dynamics are recognized and constancy maintained whenever possible.

With or without a trained receptionist these difficulties would occur, and part of the training of a counsellor in a group private practice should alert them to the likelihood of such interactions. If foreseen they can then be incorporated into the counselling process. Another predictable difficulty is that the group can become the focus of the client's anger and frustration, so that the negative feelings towards the counsellor are displaced outside the counselling relationship. Again, forewarned is forearmed, and the counsellor's task would be to help the client recognize how feelings are being displaced and disowned.

Other potential problem areas in a group practice are that messages can become garbled when they are being passed on, and that maintaining boundaries and confidentiality is a complex issue. Preventing intrusions and interruptions when more people are using a building or more than one counsellor is using a counselling room is not straightforward and needs careful attention. In all these instances special care has to be taken and it is helpful to establish regular group meetings. These are important because they also minimize the possibility of a breakdown in communication and allow differences to be discussed and conflicts to be resolved. If they are not, the clients are bound to be affected unconsciously, if not consciously, by conflict in the practice.

There are also advantages to, and difficulties in, working alone. The major advantage of working alone is autonomy. Thus counsellors are able to decide how they want to work, with whom they want to work, how much they charge, the hours they work, where they want to work, etc. One disadvantage is obvious: that is isolation, which is neither good for counsellors nor their clients, and must be counteracted. Another disadvantage could be the financial burden of creating enough revenue on one's own to service the running costs of a business, such as rental of rooms, or mortgage and rates for a building, decorating and furnishing and maintenance of counselling room(s), telephone, etc., and provide an income.

There would seem to be more advantages to working in a

group practice of counsellors than working alone, and yet in Britain at present the majority of counsellors in private practice work alone. This may well be related to the question of premises.

Whether in a group practice or working alone, premises are needed for counselling. The possibilities if working alone are to use one's own house; or to rent or buy premises, such as one or two rooms in an office block, or a house. If buying property to be used solely for the practice, it is essential to check with local planning departments that the premises can be used for this purpose. If working in a group practice, then one member of the group might have a large enough house, part of which could be converted; again, offices can be rented or bought, as can a whole house. It is fairly rare for a member of a group to own a private house, part of which could be used for the group practice. This leaves the option of renting or purchasing premises. Whether working alone or as part of a group, renting property could be a high fixed expense with perhaps little or no income to cover it, particularly when starting up; on the other hand, purchasing property may involve too big a capital outlay. Neither may be viable for a counsellor only doing a small amount of private work; it is quite common for counsellors to be both employed as a counsellor and to do a small amount of work privately. It may well be for these reasons that at present in Britain the majority of counsellors in private practice work on their own using their private home. It should be borne in mind that whenever domestic property is used partly for commercial purposes, the Local Authority should be informed as they have the right to levy extra charges.

Whichever is chosen, the prerequisites are a waiting-room, a counselling-room and a lavatory. A room for a receptionist/secretary may also be necessary. In choosing accommodation it is essential that it offers total privacy, with no possibility of being overheard and with the rooms not being overlooked. It is also important to ensure that the disabled have access.

It is essential if a counsellor decides to use her or his own house that family and clients can be kept separate. This may mean a different entrance for clients as well as a room set aside solely for counselling.

The main advantage of a counsellor using her or his own house is cost. Perhaps the only cost is the alteration of a room into a consulting-room. But in this environment certain issues can be predicted that will arise for clients precisely because they are in a private home.

First, counsellors cannot maintain the same anonymity that would exist if counselling in a room in an office block. Anonymity is usually regarded as an important aid in understanding the client, because many assumptions about the counsellor will be imaginary and derived from past experiences with key-carers. In private practice it is extremely difficult to remove all evidence of a partner and/or children and of a life-style. This will affect the material the client brings in terms of transference and projections. It could also result in envy fuelled by real knowledge as well as from transference-based assumptions. This is illustrated in the following vignette:

> Claire, a counsellor, worked in her own home, a detached house in a wealthy suburb of a large city. She had not always lived in such comfort, having been brought up in considerable poverty. For her, years of hard work were necessary before she could buy the house she now lived in.
>
> Peter, her client, constantly attacked her for her luck, saying such things as, 'You were born with a silver spoon in your mouth!'; 'You don't know what hard work is!'; 'You live very comfortably!' The last of these three accusations was actually true and could be seen by Peter.
>
> Claire felt very uncomfortable and attacked by all the accusations, and her first thoughts were, 'How dare he! Little does he know,' and then a feeling of guilt about living in such comfort.
>
> Her dilemma as a counsellor was how to use her own thoughts and feelings to help Peter recognize that there was appropriate envy and the associated pain for him because she did live in more comfortable surroundings. There were also false assumptions which gave her insight into his unconscious world, which in turn could be used to help him recognize his envy, hate and anger.

A second issue is the difficulty of preventing the family from creating distractions. Even the best behaved families have their crises! A few examples from my own household are: a major row between two of my children on the stairs outside the counselling-room, which dispelled any myth of the ideal family; a neighbour's young child who rushed straight into the house and into the counselling-room; an overflowing bidet, first noticed when drips came through the ceiling of the counselling-room. Of course, there are uncontrollable distractions wherever a counsellor works and these become material for the counselling work. However, family 'noises off' will lead to clients deducing information about the counsellor, whether these inferences are correct or not. These become integral to the process and raise issues that become part of the counselling, as the following vignette illustrates:

> My daughter and a child she was looking after entered the house through the front door. Roger, my client, did not see or hear this. Suddenly the child started crying inconsolably. He did not appear to notice this, but shortly afterwards his manner changed quite abruptly and he began attacking me viciously saying: 'You only see me because I pay you; you don't really care!'
>
> Knowing some of his childhood experiences, I suggested that my lack of response to the child crying in the house made him angry. During the remainder of the session it became clear that my lack of response to the child (whom he thought was mine) reminded him of his childhood. Gradually he remembered how angry he had felt with his mother who believed children should not be made a fuss of. She frequently left Roger crying even when he was badly frightened or hurt.

In most houses it is extremely likely that entrances will be placed so that the client cannot help but see into some of the rooms. This is another way in which clients could be affected by working in a private house. The next two vignettes illustrate how similar circumstances can be understood by clients in totally contrasting ways:

a)   One evening when Jean came for her regular appointment she saw through a window a group of seven or eight people. Jean gave me no indication that she had noticed all these people and there was no external noise. For much of the session she seemed very sullen and barely spoke. When I suggested she was angry with me this was denied. However, she started telling me about how her mother was always busy with the rest of the family and uninterested in her. Jean was

certain that I was just the same and this had been
evoked for her by seeing the people in the house.

b) It was school holidays and my children together with
their friends were congregated in the kitchen. George
could see a group of young people as he came down the
drive for his regular appointment. As he came through
the door he said, uncharacteristically, 'How good it is
to see you today.' During the session he spoke of how
his father and he had had private jokes that no one
else in the family understood. Clearly this had made
him feel very special. This feeling was evoked by seeing
me while all these young people were in the house.

It must be remembered that seeing clients in a private house
will also have effects on anyone living in the house. If a counsellor
has children living in the house, they will have to try be as quiet
and unobtrusive as possible. It is hard for them in particular
to understand why it is necessary to respect a client's need for
privacy and therefore avoid meeting clients. It is sometimes even
harder to manage not to meet a client, particularly when some
clients may actively try to see them. On occasions I have been
aware of my children's difficulty in managing a chance meeting,
such as arriving at the garden gate at the same time as a client.
Do they pretend they are not really going to that house? Or just
say 'hallo'? Or ignore the client? Or what? It is important to
rehearse with the family what they should do in these situations, so they are not uncomfortable and unnatural. Obviously
what I had thought was a request that they should avoid meeting
clients had been a very fierce order! Family members of any
counsellor have to cope with the knowledge that each client is
having an hour a week of their parent's or partner's time. This
is even more difficult to cope with when it is happening in their
own house. They will be aware that the clients are being given
uninterrupted time: something they may rarely get for themselves. This can cause a lot of additional envy in the family,
which counsellors need to recognize and understand. The following is an account of just such a reaction of a counsellor's
children:

Bridget was a single parent with two children, Sarah, who
was seven, and Tom, who was ten. She worked from home

and saw clients some evenings when the children were in the house, upstairs. Her counselling room was on the ground floor so the clients never saw the children or vice versa. The children had learnt to be very quiet and rarely disturbed the counselling work.

One evening when she had finished counselling, Bridget went upstairs to find a notice on Sarah's door. It read: NO CLINTS ALOUD. It was a clear message to Bridget that Sarah had had enough of her mother's work interfering with her life.

If counsellors work from their own homes, they are much more affected by clients or themselves making a mistake with the appointment time. Thus if they arrive unexpectedly first thing in the morning at a private house, they could be greeted by a member of the family, if not the counsellor, in their nightclothes. It has happened! This type of mistake on the client's part might be an unconscious desire to invade the counsellor's territory. When the counsellor makes such a mistake it might be denied hostility to the client, or unconscious resentment, having given the client an appointment at an inconvenient time. Should a muddle occur with appointment times when a counsellor works in an office, then clients may get no answer at all, or there may be a receptionist and no counsellor. As with all unusual occurrences the responses will give access to latent material.

Renting or buying an office offers the counsellor's household more protection and helps maintain much more anonymity for the counsellor, particularly concerning personal life-style and family circumstances. However, anonymity is never total. Clients will pick up information from the clothes a counsellor wears, how she or he speaks, and the way the waiting-room and counselling-room are decorated and arranged.

HOW COUNSELLORS IN
INDEPENDENT PRACTICE FIND CLIENTS

There are significant differences between finding clients when a independent practice is new as opposed to when it is well-established. Whatever stage a practice is at, counsellors find clients by being visible and creating trust (Kopp 1977: 24). When starting from scratch a counsellor probably has to advertise. This can be done verbally through friends and contacts but may result in friends asking for counselling. These people should never be clients. This is clearly set out in the Codes of Ethics and Practice of some counselling organizations. However, a counsellor's network of friends may produce some appropriate clients, as will giving talks about counselling whenever the opportunity arises.

Advertising more formally by producing a leaflet or a letter outlining personal details and the way one works can be useful. The BAC Code of Ethics and Practice for Counsellors specifies that when advertising, information should be limited to 'name, relevant qualifications, address, telephone number, hours available and a brief listing of services offered'. This can then be circulated to local GPs, religious organizations and voluntary organizations, such as the Samaritans, MIND and RELATE. This type of publicity is always more effective if it is followed up by a personal meeting.

Good publicity should include many of the details which should also be in a pre-counselling leaflet; indeed such a leaflet can serve both purposes. This will be mentioned in detail in Chapters 3 and 4. The following is an example of a letter which might be sent when looking for counselling work.

> Dear
> I have recently set up in independent practice as a counsellor. I am a trained counsellor (person-centred) and have been an accredited counsellor (BAC) for five years. My particular areas of expertise are in bereavement counselling and stress management.
> My working hours are from 08.30 to 18.00 on Mondays and Wednesdays, 16.00 to 22.00 on Tuesdays and Fridays and 09.00 to 13.00 on Saturdays. My fees are £x per hour.
> I would welcome the opportunity to come and discuss my work with you in more detail.
> Yours sincerely,

It is useful for a counsellor to make an entry in the directory produced by BAC and into registers of any local counselling organizations, although many of these publications are only produced annually or even biennially. Some of these directories can be very misleading because membership of an organization

or partial qualifications are presented as if they are professional
accreditation. For instance, MASC used to indicate that a counsellor is a Member of the Association for Student Counselling
(ASC, a Division of BAC). This looks impressive, but is misleading. For many professional associations 'membership' means ex-
aminations have been passed and the person is an accredited
practitioner (e.g. Member of the Institution of Mechanical Engineers; MIMechE); this is not the case in ASC. This association
does have an accreditation scheme. Any accredited member is
allowed under the statutes of the association to call themselves
an accredited student counsellor. MASC does not exist as an
acronym. Directories can also be misleading if affiliation with an
organization is presented in a way which falsely implies sponsor-
ship by the organization. Both these practices are unethical and
not allowed if a counsellor is a member of BAC.

Care has to be taken in choosing where to advertise. The
actual choice could well be dictated by whether a counsellor
works from home or in a group practice which is well-staffed.
In BAC's information sheet on Counselling in Private Practice,
counsellors are cautioned in the following way: 'You are open
to approaches from people who may be highly disturbed and
unlikely to be able to make use of counselling. For this reason
it is good practice to make it clear when the initial contact is
made, that the first meeting will be for assessment of the client's
needs before a commitment to counselling is made.' This is good
practice and will be discussed in Chapter 3. Examples of places
used to display advertisements are on notice boards in GP's
surgeries, libraries and shops, in local newspapers, and in the
Yellow Pages. Currently the latter has three categories which are
suitable: 'Counselling and Advice', 'Psychotherapy and Analysis'
and 'Therapists'. A number of counsellors have found that
advertising here has not been useful, with requests for physiotherapy, sexual harassment by phone, and clients who make
appointments they do not keep.

HOW CLIENTS FIND COUNSELLORS

Clients do find counsellors through seeing advertisements or
consulting directories produced by national organizations, such as
BAC and so are self-referred. They can also be told of counsellors

in the neighbourhood by local branches of national organizations such as RELATE or the Samaritans, or by local voluntary or work-based counselling services. Well-established counsellors find that more often their clients come by word of mouth. This may be on the recommendation of a current or an ex-client, or the more indirect route through a friend or acquaintance of past or present clients. (In my own practice 60 per cent of my present clients have reached me this way.) Of course, all clients carry expectations when they first arrive, but if the counsellor has been recommended by someone, then clients will bring a mixture of accurate facts and transference projections belonging to the referring client. These will have to be borne in mind when working with the new client. Should the referring client still be a client, it is very important to establish how the referral came about and whether the established client is aware that a friend or acquaintance is seeking counselling. It could be very significant that a client has offered his or her counsellor to a friend. Was the client a child who had to share everything with his or her brothers and sisters, and yet always resented that deeply? If this is the case it will emerge in the counselling process.

Another route to counselling is via another counsellor or therapist. Again, this will affect the expectations and feelings of new clients towards the counsellor. It is more common for counsellors to suggest names of other counsellors that might be approached than to make a formal referral. If a counsellor has given an assessment session and then said she or he felt unable to work with a client, or even if the client has decided after an assessment session that the wait until a vacancy arises is unacceptable, there will be consequences. In either case there may be resentment because 'they were not wanted'. It is even more significant in the second case where clients have set up their own 'not wantedness'.

The third 'word-of-mouth' route is that the client has attended a talk or training event given by the counsellor. If the latter is the case, the BAC Code of Ethics and Practice for Trainers stipulates that there should be a break for reflection and the supervisor should be consulted. I would recommend at least six months. Even so, the counselling relationship may be extremely difficult because the counsellor may well behave very differently when working as a trainer than when counselling. This means that the client could reasonably expect a counsellor to behave in the way they did as a trainer and be very disappointed when this does not occur, as is illustrated in the following example:

Frank had attended a course run by Mary. During a tutorial he revealed to Mary that he had been sexually abused as a child. Mary was the first person he had ever spoken to about this. Mary advised him that he should seek some counselling to help him unravel all that had happened to him. This he agreed to do. The last session of the course included overt demonstrations of affection between all the course members and the trainers.

Some months later Frank approached Mary and asked her if she would consider taking him on as a client. He had thought about approaching other counsellors, but decided that Mary would be best, as she already knew his story and he did not want to have to start again telling a stranger all the painful story. Mary was aware of how difficult it had been for Frank to tell her about the abuse and the course had finished nine months earlier, so she agreed to work with Frank.

After a short time it became clear that Frank was disappointed, angry and resentful with Mary. He was reluctant to tell Mary what was affecting him. Gradually it emerged that he had chosen Mary because he expected to be hugged. This might have been a reasonable expectation, having been on Mary's course; but it was not her way of working when counselling. Once Mary understood the misunderstanding, she could recognize Frank's disappointment and help him decide if he still wanted to work with her.

In independent, private practice it is less usual for clients to be referred. Formal referrals are made by employers/bosses, EAPs, GPs, psychiatrists, hospital *in vitro* fertilization (IVF) programmes, religious organizations, and occasionally counsellors and therapists. The issues related to these referrals will be discussed in Chapter 5.

This chapter has focused on why counsellors become independent practitioners and the particular context in which they work. The context is different in a number of ways from counsellors who are employed by an institution or company or who work voluntarily for an agency. In independent practice the client is usually the employer and therefore the counsellor the

employee. Another way to look at this is that the counsellor is
a supplier of services and the client a customer. This makes more
sense of the counsellor having to choose where to work, with
whom to work, and to find the clients. The consequences of
these choices raise special difficulties that a counsellor in independent practice must be aware of, so they can be recognized
and used in the counselling process.

In the next chapter the issues that are common to all counsellors, regardless of the context of the counselling, are looked
at in the light of the special demands of independent, private
practice.

· THREE ·

The practice of counselling in independent practice

Before the first client is even seen, all counsellors, regardless of setting, have to make careful preparations. Counsellors in agencies and working in institutions will have some of these decisions made for them. In independent practice, counsellors will have to make all decisions alone, although consultation with their supervisor would be sensible. Choice of premises and advertising have already been mentioned, but decisions also need to be made on the number of clients seen a week, the hours to be made available for counselling, the number of vacancies, who are suitable clients and how to handle unsuitable clients, and how to protect oneself. Once these decisions have been made, then counsellors are prepared to handle the first contacts and begin the actual counselling. This chapter looks at both the background decisions and then the issues common to all counsellors about pre-counselling information, the initial contact, assessment of clients, contract, records, terminating the counselling relationship, issues of race and gender, arrangements for supervision and continuing training, and 'taking care of yourself'.

CLIENT CONTACT HOURS

A basic decision for all counsellors is the number of clients they see each week. For counsellors in independent practice this will be partly controlled by the number of hours they want to work and the closely related issue of what they want to earn. A much more important issue, though, is the need to take care of themselves. I would recommend no more than five clients per day and 20 sessions with regular clients per week if working full-time. There are a number of reasons for this. The main one is highlighted by Storr (1979: 182) in writing about psychotherapists, but it is equally true for counsellors. He comments that: 'there is a danger of the therapist becoming a non-person; a prostitute parent whose children are not only illegitimate but more imaginary than real'. Storr suggests that this 'self-abnegation' should be counteracted and suggests that: 'it is essential for the therapist to find some area in which he [sic] lives for himself alone, in which self-expression . . . is demanded'. Storr then quotes suggestions for analysts from Szasz (1965: 219) of 'teaching, research or writing'. All these activities are possible for counsellors, assuming they have the necessary training and motivation. Other suggestions include belonging to a journal club or to a counsellor-support group.

Another reason for a limit to the amount of work each day, and the number of hours with regular clients, is the additional time needed for assessment sessions, emergency sessions (if this is on offer), the return of old clients (if this is on offer), and for offering a client two sessions each week rather than one session each week for a period of time (see later in this chapter). Counsellors also need time for some office work, making notes, their own training and supervision and possibly their own counselling or therapy. Finally, if counsellors are sufficiently experienced and suitably qualified, they may wish to be supervisors for other counsellors.

The majority of counsellors and psychotherapists see their clients once a week, or at most twice a week, rather than three to five times a week, which is normal psychoanalytic practice. This difference in practice has occurred for a number of reasons. There is no evidence that very intensive therapy is any more successful than once-a-week therapy (Storr 1979: x). The majority of people can neither afford the time nor the money for intensive therapy, and intensive therapy would severely limit the number of people that can be helped at any one time. The norm of one session a week makes sense both economically and psychologically. When counsellors conduct an assessment session with potential clients they have to decide (among other issues) whether clients have sufficient 'ego-strength' to be able to use one or two sessions a week, implying an ability to continue some of the exploration from a session on their own. It is usual to offer a client one session a week at the beginning, with the possibility of increasing to twice a week later, if the counsellor in consultation with a supervisor, and with the agreement and understanding of the client, consider this to be therapeutically necessary.

HOURS AVAILABLE

It is unlikely, regardless of whether working full-time or part-time, that the conventional 'office' working hours of 09.00 to 17.00, Monday to Friday, could accommodate client demand or create enough income for a counsellor. Clients frequently want to come either before their working day starts or at the end. This means that sessions starting at 08.30 and 17.00 are much sought after, as are evening sessions or Saturday sessions. Of course, many people do have some flexibility of working hours, as flexitime becomes increasingly common. It is also possible that creating difficulties about the timing of sessions is evidence of a client's ambivalence about counselling. None the less there are people who are unable to come for counselling during their working hours. Obviously, counsellors have to decide what hours they want to work, and if they decide to work evenings or weekends then they need to timetable free time at other times. Unless this decision is a firm and active one, it is all too easy to overwork.

Occasionally counsellors are asked if they would counsel the client in the client's own home. Sometimes this request comes from lack of knowledge and perhaps from equating a counsellor with a GP. There will be occasions when the person would not be able to get to a counsellor's premises. A current trend, for instance, is for cancer patients to seek counselling, particularly if they have been in contact with the Bristol Cancer Help Centre or with the British Association of Cancer United Patients (BACUP). These patients may be too ill to travel. From a counsellor's point of view it is important to have already decided in principle whether she or he is trained to do this type of work and prepared to travel to a client's house. The travelling will obviously take time and might be very difficult to timetable into a working day with commitments of an hour at a time to regular clients. If a decision is made to be prepared to travel, then if the travelling, as well as counselling time, is charged for, it could be prohibitively expensive for the client. This is a difficult decision that can only be made on a personal basis.

PRE-COUNSELLING INFORMATION

Before ever meeting a counsellor, clients are likely to have seen publicity about counselling, or sought information from the counsellor over the telephone or in writing. This pre-counselling information should 'reflect accurately the nature of the service on offer, and the training, qualifications and relevant experience of the counsellor (BAC Code of Ethics and Practice for Counsellors, Clause B2.2.8)'. The information is best presented in a leaflet that can be sent to anyone who enquires about counselling and also to a client before meeting for an assessment session. Apart from clarifying what clients are committing themselves to if they decide to enter a counselling relationship, it also enables clients to compare counsellors before even asking for an assessment session, and to choose the counsellor who seems to offer the greatest experience and safeguards. A good pre-counselling leaflet should include:

Name, address and telephone number of counsellor;
Hours available;
Relevant training and qualifications; membership of professional organizations;
Years of experience;
Whether counsellor has received or is receiving personal counselling or therapy;
Whether work is supervised or not;
Code of Ethics and Practice adhered to;
Complaints procedure;
Brief listing of services offered;
Explanation of what counselling involves;
Examples of issues that are appropriate to bring to counselling;
Fees payment and cancellation procedure;
Use of assessment session(s) for both counsellor and prospective client to decide whether to proceed with counselling;

How to arrange an assessment session;
Directions for finding counselling premises.

An example of a pre-counselling leaflet is given in Appendix A.
It is increasingly likely that clients will begin to expect this
amount of detail. A number of articles in the press (see Chapters
4 and 6) in recent years have detailed the questions a person
ought to be asking when looking for a counsellor. A pre-
counselling leaflet will pre-empt such requests and simultaneously educate people about what they ought to expect. Another
result of these newspaper and magazine articles, and also the
initiative of the Conservative government in publishing the Citi-
zen's Charter and the Patient's Charter, is a demand for a Client's Charter. A pre-counselling leaflet might also be used for
this purpose. Bond (forthcoming) quotes extensively from such
a charter published by York and Scarborough College and Nurse
Counselling Network. The charter addresses three main areas.
These are what a client has a right to, what a client can expect
and the client's responsibility. These issues are treated in a different way by a group of psychotherapists in Sheffield. Apart
from a leaflet given to anyone enquiring about psychotherapy,
they give each client a booklet (Oram 1987) and another leaflet
at the end of the initial assessment session. The booklet describes
psychotherapy, and outlines what a commitment to therapy
would involve. It also illustrates how a therapy relationship differs
from a conventional social relationship. The leaflet gives the cost
of therapy and outlines what a client may 'reasonably expect in
return for the outlay of a fee'. Five expectations are listed and
elaborated. These are: the therapist's undivided, albeit limited,
time; skills and experience; honesty and integrity; genuine
concern; reliability.

INITIAL CONTACT

I suggested in the previous section that pre-counselling leaflets
could be sent in response to an initial enquiry, whether by telephone or letter. In fact a letter of enquiry is extremely rare in
my experience and initial contact is most likely to be by telephone. The majority of clients seem to ring expecting an appointment, perhaps because this is the system in a GP's surgery.

As a result it is more likely that the pre-counselling leaflet will be sent when confirming the date and time of the assessment session.

Obviously this phone call will be extremely important and counsellors need to be prepared for it for three main reasons. These are to protect themselves from overwork and from unsuitable clients, and to create the beginnings of a predictable environment. This latter containment is one of the main features of a good counselling relationship.

Two ways of preventing overwork have been mentioned. These are knowing the maximum number of clients that can be taken and restricting the working hours. The third is a result of the first two. At some point there are no vacancies and either clients are turned away (Kopp 1977: 31) or a waiting-list must be started. In an established practice there is usually a waiting list, which may be as long as six months. Clients need to be warned of this, but the counsellor has to decide whether to offer a potential client an assessment session close to the first enquiry, or once a vacancy is foreseen.

The advantage of an assessment earlier rather than later is that potential clients have met the counsellor and found out what they need to know, to enable them to make comparisons between different counsellors and decide who they wish to work with. Simultaneously the counsellor can assess, using the normal criteria, which are discussed later in this chapter, and inform potential clients whether she or he will be able and want to work with them once a vacancy arises. The reasons for deciding not to work with a client are varied. Perhaps the most frequent ones are either that the counsellor believes that the person seeking counselling would not be helped, or that he or she cannot help the person. Whatever the reason, it is important to be honest and if it is the latter give guidance on how to find other counsellors. For many potential clients an assessment session is sufficient to 'keep them going' until a vacancy arises, assuming that both the counsellor and client have agreed to work together. For a few, the experience of waiting, having met the counsellor, has a teasing quality, which they may not be able to handle. It is important to talk about the timing of assessment in the initial phone call and then let potential clients decide for themselves whether to proceed now or later. The majority decide on a fairly early assessment session before joining the waiting-list. Inevitably the wait means a few have changed their mind or recovered by the time a vacancy arises for them.

It was mentioned in the last chapter that advertising is likely to result in requests from people who are totally unsuitable for counselling or unsuitable if a counsellor works alone in a private house. Before any potential client makes contact, a counsellor must decide what clients are suitable and have rehearsed methods of turning away the unsuitable. Highly disturbed people, those with personality disorders and those who are violent are all unsuitable. It is not always possible to determine unsuitability from a telephone conversation, which means care must be taken by counsellors to ensure that they are protected. This can be done by never seeing a new client when alone in a building, having an alarm system in the certain knowledge that someone will respond, and making it clear that the assessment session carries with it no obligation to continue seeing someone.

The first impression obtained from the telephone conversation is the initial step in creating a firm and secure framework for the whole counselling relationship. It is important, therefore, to have a check-list of what a client making an appointment for an assessment session needs to know by the end of this conversation. The following points, some of which are also stated in the pre-counselling leaflet, need to be mentioned:

Whether there is a vacancy, and if not how long before a vacancy arises;

The effects of having an assessment straight away or once a vacancy arises;

Working hours, and session times available;

Description of the aims of an assessment session;

Clarification that an assessment session allows both parties to choose whether to proceed to a counselling relationship or not;

Length of assessment session;

Fees for an assessment session;

Fees for a normal counselling session;

Date and time of assessment session;

Instructions about car-parking (if relevant);

Policy about answering the door and what will happen if they arrive too early or late;

Arrangements about the waiting-room (if there is one);

Clear request that if the client decides not to proceed he/she

should inform the counsellor by letter or telephone and in good time (non-attendance with no notification is common at this stage);
Check client knows counsellor's address, telephone number and how to find the counselling premises;
Check client's address and telephone number.

The reasons for most of these points are self-evident. Some need elaboration, particularly those related to answering the door and arrangements about the waiting-room and car-parking. The majority of clients have never been to a counsellor before and understandably treat coming to a counsellor like going to their GP. The result is that they do not expect to be seen at their precise appointment time. Some arrive very early, perhaps because of a combination of anxiety over finding a new place and about 'getting things right'. Others arrive late, perhaps hoping that they will have least waiting-time. Both these approaches play havoc with a counselling session where both the start and finish time are firmly held. Clients must, therefore, be clear about the consequences of arriving late or early. The early arrival causes an additional problem for the counsellor who has no receptionist and who has a policy of not leaving a client to answer the door. If there is a receptionist and a waiting-room then clients can be let into the premises and wait. If there is no receptionist and the counsellor's policy is not to leave a client, then the new client needs to know this.

It may sound controlling to give clients instructions about car-parking. A new client may not have thought about other clients and their need for privacy. Again this may be because when going to a GP the only privacy is in the consulting room. The car-park and waiting-room are open to all. If clients come by car, arrive early and know there is no waiting-room and that the counsellor does not answer the door when working, then they will wait in their car outside the counselling premises until the appointment time. For some premises this may result in their seeing the previous client leaving, which invades the privacy of that client and, of course, of the new client. A new client therefore needs to be asked not to park outside the premises until a few minutes before the appointment time.

Another consequence of clients assuming that going to a GP

and a counsellor are similar is that some people assume that the front door will be unlocked and they can just walk into the building, without knocking, and sit down. This can be most disconcerting. If a counsellor has a waiting-room and works in a building which has open access, then the new client needs to know this. If the counselling-room is in private premises and there is no receptionist, then, for safety reasons, the main door should be locked and clients need to know that they cannot get access to the building until say ten minutes before the appointment time.

If the initial contact is by telephone, it is good practice to follow up this call by sending the pre-counselling leaflet and a letter (Appendix B) or another leaflet with the additional information discussed in the telephone call. This letter or leaflet would confirm the actual appointment time; give procedures if a client arrives early, the consequences of late arrival and practical arrangements related to reception, the waiting-room and car-parking; and a request that should a client decide not to proceed, then he or she should make a cancellation in good time.

While it costs money to have such a leaflet printed and posted, it has two important functions. First, it removes some of the anxiety for the client about doing something new, so the beginnings of a secure base are put in place. Second, a telephone conversation can be misremembered, reinterpreted, imagined or forgotten. If the main things said are also written down, then both client and counsellor know exactly where they are. For the counsellor this means that any discrepancy between what the client was told and now remembers, certainly signals the anxiety of a new client and may possibly give access to unconscious processes.

ASSESSMENT

The broad aim of assessment is to discover what a client is looking for and to match it with what can be offered. It is the same for all counsellors regardless of their work context. However, counsellors in independent practice are not constrained in what they can offer by such things as mission statements of the employing institution (an example is: 'to support the institute of higher education in its primary function of providing higher education'); job descriptions and restrictions on areas of work imposed by an 'external' body, be it employer or voluntary agency (examples are: 'Anyone asking for help must be seen within 48 hours, and clients may be offered a maximum of eight sessions'). In independent practice, constraints are self-imposed. Counsellors decide for themselves and take the responsibility for the number of client-contact hours; the clients they work with; the areas they specialize in; the balance of short-term and long-term work; how they handle a waiting-list (if they have one); and whether they take emergency referrals or only offer emergency sessions to established clients. They also have the luxury of not having to see everyone unlike many employed counsellors.

It should be easy to operate a waiting-list once a decision has been made to have one. However, discussion with other counsellors in the private sector and my own experience reveal that certain clients do manage to by-pass the waiting list. It is obviously important to understand why this occurs, as it gives clues about a client. It may be that she or he is very demanding or very needy, and in either case this has been irresistible for the counsellor. Often with such a client the assessment session never happens and counselling starts immediately. The following is an account of such an interaction.

> I received a phone call from a Mr Brown, who told me he had just taken over the job of organizer of a local advice bureau. I knew that his predecessor had often made good referrals to me in the past, so when he said he would like to meet me I arranged an appointment for the following week. After I had put the phone down I realized I was not clear about why he was coming to see me. Was he coming to meet me so he would know to whom he was referring people? Or was he coming for his own needs?
>
> When he arrived he launched straight into his own problems and clearly was expecting to go straight into a counselling relationship. He had had counselling before he moved job and house. At no point in this first session was I able to say that I had not been clear about the aim of this meeting. Despite no assessment session and a waiting-list, Mr Brown was now a client.

More normally there is an assessment session. In private, independent practice the assessment session is usually made by the counsellor who will work with the client. The exception to this is in a small number of group practices where any one of the members of the group might make the assessment and then a group decision will be taken on the allocation of a client to a counsellor. Another method of working, common in a number of agencies, is for one member of the group to make all the assessments and also to be responsible for the subsequent allocation to the counsellors in the group. When working alone the assessment has to be done with considerable care, particularly in the area of predicting the possibility of violent behaviour and other kinds of acting out. These sessions are usually longer than counselling sessions: an hour and a half is common. Even then a second session may be necessary because counsellors may wish to consult with either their own supervisor or a client's GP or psychiatrist, before making the decision of whether to offer a client counselling.

The assessment has a similar structure regardless of the context of the counselling. First, counsellors have to establish why a client has decided to look for counselling, what outcome is hoped for and whether counselling is appropriate to meet this aim. Second, counsellors discover whether a client is psychologically-minded. This is done by offering a psychological explanation and seeing how this is understood and used. Third, a counsellor has to hear the client's life-history to check whether the client has lived through particular life-events and emotional experiences which would suggest early emotional damage. This information enables the counsellor to decide whether a recent crisis has led a client to seek counselling or whether there is a long-term history of emotional damage or a combination of both. The life-history may also contain information, such as long periods of psychiatric treatment, which would be a contra-indication to counselling. If there are contra-indications, counsellors should decide not to do any in-depth work and possibly offer some short-term support or advise the person against counselling. Short-term support would be appropriate for an elderly person whose partner had just died, whereas if the person has a history of several breakdowns and a partner had just died, it would be sensible to advise against counselling and suggest he or she seeks help from a GP or psychiatrist. If there are no contra-indications the counsellor has to decide whether short-term work is appropriate or long-term in-depth work is most suitable. Short-term work would be the choice where the client has a history of stable relationships and no major losses before late teenage. Long-term in-depth work would be the preference where, for example, a client has had a number of events in early life (under 12) which had elements of abandonment or rejection, such as being hospitalized without parental accompaniment for a week as a two-year-old, or having had a mother who had bouts of clinical depression, or a parent who died.

Every assessment session is a two-way process. There will be questions that clients need to ask, apart from those mentioned in the section on pre-counselling information. These centre around what counselling or therapy will achieve, and how long it will take. As early as 1928 Ferenczi discussed this, making it clear that clients must know that there are other methods of treatment which may 'hold out quicker and more definite prospects of a cure' (Ferenczi 1928/1955: 87). Clients may well have doubts about counselling or therapy and the likelihood of success. Ferenczi stressed that clients need to understand therapy as a 'bold experiment, which will cost . . . a great deal of toil, time and money'. He goes on to stress that clients must decide for themselves 'whether or not the amount of suffering which [their] difficulties are causing [them] is sufficient to make the experiment worth while in spite of all that'. This is still good advice. Clients must decide for themselves, with no pressure from their counsellors, that they want to take the risk of counselling, when no guarantee can be given of the time needed or the outcome.

The last but not least important stage of an assessment is for counsellors to decide whether they have the knowledge, skills and experience to do the required work. If not they should refer a client to someone else, giving the client clear reasons for this decision.

It is at this point that counsellors in independent, private prac-tice may have much greater freedom than employed counsellors. They only have their own self-imposed restrictions about the depth and duration of work, so they are totally free to offer long-term work if they consider it necessary, and have the training, skills, experience and ability and if the client can afford it. Where the client cannot afford the long-term work the options are to suggest a counselling agency that accepts either a contribution or charges no fee (if there is one in the neighbourhood), or there may be other counsellors who charge lower fees, have some concessionary places or have a sliding scale. It is not appropriate to start work in the hope that the money will be found, or working fortnightly if the counsellor has already assessed that weekly sessions would be the correct level of interaction. In some instances, the refusal by the counsellor to work for a limited time results in clients realizing that it is not lack of funds that has led them to stipulate that they only have enough money for say ten weeks, but their own commitment problems.

Before undertaking such long-term work counsellors in independent practice need to assess their own abilities. This work might involve considerable regression and dependency, which demands much more support and time than is usual. There may be times when a client becomes so regressed that they need more sessions each week than have been agreed at the outset. Sometimes they are so much in touch with the child in themselves that they need the 'cradle rocked between sessions'. This can be done by phone. Special arrangements may also have to be made when the counsellor is on holiday or ill. It is clear that a counsellor can only manage one client at a time with this level of need; hence the necessity of knowing quite precisely the different demands of other clients currently in counselling. It is also essential that counsellors are well-supported by their supervisor when undertaking this type of work. In this instance the supervision offers the counsellor something akin to the ego support which Winnicott (1972: 43) suggested a father gives to a nursing mother. Though whether Winnicott would make such an observation nowadays, with fathers being much more involved in infant care, is debatable.

Many counsellors in the independent sector do a disproportionate amount of long-term work compared to their counterparts in, for example, a student counselling service. If I look at my own practice, the average time for counselling is about two years, ranging from a few weeks to many years. Nearly half stay more than two years, a quarter between one and two years and the rest less than a year. Some reasons for this will be discussed in more detail in Chapter 4.

Assessment sessions not only enable counsellors to decide whether they can work with a client and what type of work they should offer. They also allow the opportunity to consider the dangers or difficulties that might be anticipated. All counsellors are vulnerable to violent or seductive clients, but counsellors in their own home or alone in an office are in most danger. A cardinal rule is *never* to arrange a first session unless there is at a minimum a reliable alarm for an emergency, but preferably there should be someone else in the building. This offers more safety to both counsellor and client. It can be difficult to foresee the likelihood of violent behaviour, not least because clients tend to be 'on their best behaviour' at a first session. There is also no guarantee that a person will not turn out to be violent although liaison with the client's GP, provided the client has given permission for this, could establish whether there are any contra-indications which might make counselling inappropriate. Only after this has been checked should a contract for counselling work be drawn up and the work started.

A further safeguard used by some counsellors to protect themselves from inappropriate client behaviour is only to accept clients who are referred and known by another professional, a counselling colleague or a voluntary agency. In fact, this is no protection against sudden and uncharacteristic violence or a sexual proposition, but it does provide a counsellor in independent practice with a network of contacts which counteracts some of the difficulty of working alone.

CONTRACTS

All counsellors need to make a clear agreement, or contract, between themselves and their client on how they are going to work. This is usually verbal and is drawn up during or after an assessment. For a counsellor in independent practice this contract is legally binding, even though it may not be a written contract, because money is paid for a service. In most other areas of counselling, where no money changes hands, the contract might more appropriately be seen as a service agreement.

The contract must include information on:

a) The frequency and length of sessions;
b) A minimum number or in some cases a maximum number of sessions;
c) A guarantee that the counsellor will be present for the whole of an appointment, whether or not the client appears;
d) Use of telephone and letters;
e) Financial arrangements for sessions, telephone and letters;

f) Arrangements for the notification of change in fees;

g) Arrangements about cancellation for both parties, including the financial arrangements if a client misses a session;

h) The boundaries of confidentiality; with special mention (where necessary) of arrangements with the client's GP, psychiatrist or employer;

i) Information on whether notes are made or not and confirmation that, if they are made, they are securely stored and separated from any identifiable names.

In addition counsellors may want to add information about specific situations that could arise and which have been discussed during the assessment session, such as:

j) The possibility of using audio- or video-tapes to record a session as a means for the counsellor of monitoring his or her work (see Chapter 6);

k) Termination may be initiated by the counsellor if the client engages in behaviour that is unacceptable, such as harming the counsellor or the counsellor's belongings (Kopp 1977: 49);

l) A requirement that unless there is a valid reason a client should negotiate an ending with the counsellor rather than stopping abruptly. This would be made in the recognition that some of the most difficult but important work arises when a client feels so angry he or she would rather walk out than explore the source of the anger. Another reason for making such a requirement would be the recognition that negotiating an ending is immensely important in any work associated with 'loss' (Kopp 1977: 50);

m) An undertaking by the counsellor that if the time of a session has to be altered owing to changed circumstances of the counsellor then he or she will undertake, wherever possible, to offer a replacement session;

n) An undertaking by the counsellor that if the client's circumstances change he or she will make every effort to accommodate the change, but if unable to do so then the counsellor cannot be held responsible for the breaking of the contract.

In independent practice some points need further elaboration because of the payment of a fee. These issues will be discussed in Chapter 4.

Although most counsellors only make a verbal contract, it is good practice to have a leaflet which specifies the contract, including the fees and the associated issues (Appendix C). This can be used as a check-list to ensure that clients have all the information they need. Without such a list it is all too easy to leave something out and thus retain power over the client by knowing something they do not. In order to work psychodynamically and to interpret clients' behaviour so that they understand what is happening, a counsellor needs to know what a client knows. For instance, if a client is angry about a cancellation fee, this can only be interpreted when the counsellor is sure of what the client initially knew. A leaflet ensures that the information has been given, even if it has subsequently been forgotten.

CONTAINMENT

Perhaps the most important feature of counselling and psychotherapy is containment. This means offering a framework of a secure, reliable and predictable environment in which the client can feel safe and build up trust. This safe base is usually achieved by the counsellor who establishes clear boundaries for both her or himself and the client, is reliable over time-limits and frequency of meetings, makes clear arrangements about holidays, cancellations, fees, etc., and responds predictably to the client. Much of this has already been mentioned.

In independent practice it can sometimes be difficult to negotiate counselling sessions on the same day of the week and at the same time. For some clients the reality is that they work shifts, or they have jobs which require them to travel at home or abroad, or the demands made on their time are unpredictable (for instance, a solicitor who may have to remain in court until a case is heard). This means that counsellors have to be reasonable and adaptable if they take on such clients for counselling. On the other hand, it sometimes becomes clear that there is latent content in the inability of a client to negotiate a regular time for sessions. An example of this follows:

Ann worked as a nurse. She insisted that the shift system meant she could only book sessions from week to week. This meant her counsellor, George, had to accommodate her each week, often putting himself out considerably in the process. Following a supervision session, George began to realize how angry he felt with Ann. He determined to explore with her what it meant to her to have him at her beck and call. George and his supervisor thought it likely that Ann was angry with George but could only express it indirectly. In the next session Ann denied that she was angry with George, but acknowledged that she never felt that her mother was available when she needed her. By the end of this session she did admit that she knew her work-times at least a month in advance and did then plan her sessions for the whole month.

This example illustrates that while the counsellor may well have to be reasonable and accommodate the client's needs as far as is possible, it is important to be on the look-out for a hidden agenda related to the transference. There will be consequences whenever the original contract is changed.

ISSUES OF CLASS AND RACE

Fee-paying in the independent, private sector tends to mean that clients are white and middle-class, if defined in terms of income and occupation. Private clients certainly are not representative of society in racial or socioeconomic terms. If they were, about 5 per cent of clients would be from ethnic minorities; 47 per cent of clients would be employed in the professions, or employers themselves or work in managerial posts, and 53 per cent would be employed in manual jobs.

Many counsellors in the independent sector endeavour to ensure that low income does not exclude clients. They do this in a number of ways, which will be discussed in more detail in the next chapter. One way is to negotiate fees on the basis of earnings: 'robbing Peter to pay Paul'. This presupposes the client gives accurate information. However, this practice is only possible provided there are enough high-earners to balance out the low-earners. In addition, it is essential to make it clear at the first meeting that there is a sliding scale or else clients paying the top fee have every reason to feel aggrieved if they find out that others are paying less.

Another way of reducing costs for the client is to be flexible on length of session, for instance shortening sessions from an hour to 45 minutes. Or it might be possible to see a client less frequently so that the limited resources can be spread out over a longer time. This should only be agreed to if it does not jeopardize the effectiveness of the counselling.

Some clients actually state that they have budgeted a sum of money for counselling. Having established how many sessions they can 'buy' they then ask for counselling within that time limitation. There are particular skills for time-limited and focused work, and if the counsellor does not have them, the client should be referred to someone who has.

Pragmatic though they are, these approaches do not address an important issue – that most counsellors in the UK are middle-class and white and so are their clients. In private practice this might be expected, but it is also true for counselling in general. One reason for the low uptake of counselling among the ethnic minorities is that the traditional family-support systems are better, and the extended family more likely still to exist. Another reason may be that in some cultures self-sufficiency is seen as a virtue, and depression may not even be recognized. In Asian communities, in particular, health visitors find there is a reluctance to accept that post-natal depression exists. As a result, neither medical, nor psychological or counselling help is sought. While not everyone needs counselling nor is counselling for everyone, it is disturbing that it is mainly used by one band of society. This suggests that counselling and its accompanying ethos is ethnocentric.

There is, however, an increasing number of Afro-Caribbean and Asian counsellors, who are developing a style of counselling appropriate to their cultures. Some have already moved into the independent sector, and, as the numbers grow it is likely that more will do so. This should result in more people from the ethnic minorities seeking counselling in the private sector.

One way to encourage a wider representation of the 'classes' among clients would be to set up a counselling practice in the neighbourhood of that particular group. There is no doubt that it can be intimidating for some people to go to a private house in the wealthy suburb of a big city. An office can be much more impersonal and thus acceptable.

Counselling in private practice, private medicine and private schools are mainly used by the middle classes. There will have to be a radical change in the political and social ethos of the UK for this to alter. One way in which it may do so is for there to be a system of financial credits. In such a system each person would be allocated the same number of financial credits which they could then use as they wished for public or private services such as schooling and health (including counselling). The practitioners would then cash in the credits to create their revenue. At the moment such an egalitarian solution is a long way off.

KEEPING RECORDS

An inevitable part of running any business, for that is what counselling in the independent sector is, is that records need to be kept. The ethical issues related to record-keeping are dealt with in some detail by Bond (forthcoming). At the very least there must be records of clients' names, addresses and telephone numbers. Counsellors may not keep these on computer file unless they are registered under the Data Protection Act, which is a simple procedure but does cost money. However, a basic card index or book is quite adequate. Another essential is an accounting system that enables a counsellor to identify a client, while maintaining confidentiality, so that payments from clients can be entered into the accounts and checked later (see Chapter 4). Most practising counsellors also keep notes of the counselling sessions to enable them to follow the counselling process, and for use in supervision. All these records and notes must be kept securely and clients' identities protected.

Clients have a right to expect counsellors to keep their identity confidential. Indeed, there will have been some agreement on this in the initial contract. It is imperative that all information is kept as securely as possible. Should the worst happen, such as a burglary, then it should be as difficult as possible for anyone to use stolen information and to link it to a client. Obviously all information must be kept locked in filing cabinets. It is also important to separate names from addresses and from other records, and to keep them in a different location. One way to do this is to assign each client a code number. From that point on, only a code number is ever seen against an address or telephone number, on notes or in accounts. The only remaining

problem is where to keep the key to the code, again as securely
as possible.

Clients have no legal right of access to any written notes,
unless a counsellor works in a medical practice. However, counsellors should inform clients that they keep notes (BAC Code of
Ethics and Practice for Counsellors, B2.2.14). The question of
whether clients should, if they request, be given access to their
notes is discussed in some detail by Bond (forthcoming). He
suggests that notes are 'justifiably private' if they are 'merely
the counsellor's personal working notes which are never seen
by anyone else'. He goes on to observe that such detail as the
timing of the request may indicate to the counsellor that it is
transference material and needs interpretation rather than action.
Indeed, access to the notes might disrupt the counselling process.
Other counsellors might judge that there is no good reason for
keeping notes secret. As with other issues, the decision will
depend on a counsellor's theoretical background.

The legal situation is quite different if any information is kept
on computer. The Data Protection Act (1984) stipulates that
someone's name can only be on computer file if she or he has
given written permission. If information on clients is kept on
computer, it is perhaps sensible to devise a standard request
form. Clients can then be asked to read and sign it, if they agree
to their name being kept on disc. If in any doubt about the
current situation, standard leaflets on the subject should be
checked.

Counsellors must keep all records of their sessions with clients
for at least six years. If a counsellor is a member of BAC then
complaints may be lodged for up to three years from the event
which forms the substance of the complaint. Other complaints
procedures will have similar time bars. If the complaint involves
a dispute about fees then a client may instigate legal proceedings
retrospectively for as far back as six years, after which it is statute
barred. The most complex area is if a client believes that work
with a counsellor caused a medical injury, in the case of
counsellors this would be a recognized mental illness. In this
instance the client has to lodge a formal complaint within three
years of the recognition that the mental illness was caused by
the counselling. Obviously this means that counsellors should
keep all records for as long as is practicable and six years is a
minimum period.

SUPERVISION, SUPPORT AND TRAINING

In discussing client-contact hours at the beginning of this chapter I suggested that it is important to allow time for training, supervision and 'taking care of yourself'. Indeed Hawkins and Shohet (1989: 5) suggest that 'supervision can be a very important part of taking care of oneself'.

In independent practice 'taking care of oneself' becomes very real because a counsellor has to make time for supervision and organize it without the encouragement, support or pressure from others. This means selecting and employing a supervisor. Supervision is an essential part of being a practising counsellor. Indeed, a member of BAC is in breach of the Code of Ethics and Practice for Counsellors 'to practise without regular counselling supervision'. From this it is quite clear that supervision is obligatory. Frequency is often related to client load. Although BAC requires a minimum of one and a half hours supervision per *month* for accreditation purposes, many would hold this to be too little, particularly if working full-time (15–21 client contact hours). A better minimum would be one and a half hours per *fortnight* of one-to-one supervision (supervisor-counsellor model). Needless to say, a supervisor should be more experienced than the supervisee, have considerable counselling experience (ten years minimum) and have had training in supervision. Training can be from a formal course although many learn through an apprentice system. There is now a small group of BAC Accredited Supervisors (43 in March 1993).

It is sometimes held that the more experienced the counsellor, the less supervision is necessary. It is quite clear that BAC sees supervision as essential for any practising counsellor whatever their experience. I do not believe that experience justifies any lessening of the frequency of supervision, because it is 'an indispensable part of a helper's ongoing self-development, self-awareness and commitment to learning' (Hawkins and Shohet 1989: 5), quite apart from its role in self-monitoring. In many ways the necessity for supervision is even more critical for a counsellor in a single-handed independent practice. Such work can lead to isolation. This can easily lead to a drop in standards where there is no challenge from sharing and evaluating the counselling work. Isolation can also be overcome by forming a network with other counsellors or therapists in the neighbourhood to compare work and share current issues and common problems.

A further consequence of deciding to practise privately is that counsellors carry the responsibility for their own continuing professional and self-development. All additional training, whether from workshops, courses or conferences, will have to be funded out of the counsellor's own resources. A local counselling organization may meet this need, and, where they organize workshops and seminars, this could reduce the expense.

In private practice 'taking care of yourself' means arranging one's own supervision, support and training. All three contribute to personal and professional development. By neglecting this a counsellor behaves irresponsibly to her or himself, to clients and to the profession. Clients should have the safeguard of knowing that counsellors look after themselves, partly because it models self-awareness and self-respect, partly because the client does not fear quite as much that he or she will do irreparable damage to the counsellor.

TERMINATION

A counselling contract will come to an end, planned or unplanned. Ideally it will be planned and expected by both counsellor and client because they both believe that the work is complete. As a result the ending and the grief associated with the loss of the relationship will be an integral part of the counselling. Even so, it is common for both the counsellor and the client to agree that if a life-crisis occurs, or if there is more work to be done, the client may return for more counselling, assuming she or he thinks it would be helpful and the counsellor has a vacancy. This type of agreement is less common in student counselling, for instance, where the structure of academic life means that a client is only a student of a particular institute for a finite number of years. If the ex-student does require more counselling later, she or he cannot return to the student counselling service and will have to seek counselling either through a work-based counselling service, from a volunteer agency or in the private sector.

For the independent practitioner this means that a decision has to be made when planning work-schedules whether to leave a space for returning ex-clients. If the first counselling contract has enabled clients 'to enlarge' the 'understanding' of themselves 'and so to make better decisions' (Sutherland, J. D. quoted in Wallis 1973: 6) then it is likely that they will only need a few sessions. To allow for this one session a week should be kept clear. It will not be needed every week for returners and may well have several other uses, such as an emergency session for clients, a session for an emergency referral, an assessment session or simply welcome free time for the counsellor.

Termination may also be planned but unexpected for the client when, for example, the counsellor moves house to another city or town (see Chapter 4) or is pregnant. In this case the ending might be earlier than expected, but the counsellor's withdrawal can be planned and a referral made. Needless to say, the new counsellor may well have to facilitate further mourning and may also find that he or she is perceived as either not coming up to the standard of, or is 'much better' than, the previous counsellor. All of this can be worked with to help clients understand themselves and their response to abandonment or rejection.

Endings can, of course, be planned by the client and take a counsellor by surprise. A counsellor may realize that this timing is right for the client, but in some instances it may not be right in the light of the counsellor's assessment of the client's needs. When an ending is sudden and unplanned, the counsellor should take it to supervision to help him or her with the grief of this ending without a goodbye. On occasions a letter to the ex-client can be helpful to both parties. Such a letter might highlight the work done together, wish the ex-client well and round off the relationship.

Finally, termination could be unexpected and sudden for the client. This could be as the result of the sudden illness or even the death of the counsellor. A consequence of the caretaking role of counsellors is that they must have made arrangements so that, in the unlikely event of an abrupt ending to counselling, contingency plans exist. In the case of sudden illness the counsellor's family, close friends, or colleagues should know whom to contact. This might be the supervisor or another counsellor, whose task would be to inform clients and find counsellors to facilitate the grieving until the client is able to transfer to another counsellor or until ready to terminate.

The existence of such an arrangement is even more important

should a counsellor die. This is particularly so for counsellors in independent practice, whether working in a group practice or alone. They have no institutional support to assist the clients. Trayner and Clarkson (1992) suggest that even though counsellors in a group practice will have other members of the practice who can take charge, arranging support and referral, none the less all counsellors should include in their current legal will 'instructions for the termination of their practice and appropriate care for clients'. The choice of a counsellor/psychotherapist executor has to be made with care and should be discussed in advance with the person chosen. It is ill-advised for counsellors to choose a person who would be very grief-stricken by the death. On the other hand, the person has to be familiar with and sympathetic to the ways of working of the dead counsellor (Trayner and Clarkson 1992). A counsellor's supervisor might be the most appropriate person. The likely tasks for such an executor would be first to inform clients as quickly as possible and to find a counsellor who is able to facilitate the bereavement work until the client is ready to be referred to another counsellor or to terminate. There would then be notes on clients and sometimes personal material of clients to be destroyed or returned to the client, whichever is more appropriate. There may also be tapes that need to be wiped. In addition, unpaid accounts, invoices and receipts must be forwarded to the counsellor's accountant for action, though this will normally be done by the executor(s) and/or solicitor. It is probably easier to appoint the counsellor psychotherapist executor in the legal will and then give the executor(s) and/or solicitor written instructions on the procedures to follow with clients, past and present, in the event of one's death.

This chapter has looked at the counselling issues that counsellors, regardless of their context of work, have in common. The next chapter looks at issues that are unique to independent practice, such as the necessary qualifications, the use of the telephone, the management of absences, fees, insurance, accounts and taxation.

· FOUR ·

Specific issues in counselling in independent practice

The previous chapter identified general issues in counselling that are common to all counsellors regardless of the context of their work, even if for counsellors in independent practice they may have to be handled in particular ways. There are, however, many issues which are specific. In some instances, counsellors working in other contexts may find that some aspects of independent practice may give insights into their own work.

QUALIFICATIONS AND EXPERIENCE

One of the features of independent practice is that the counsellor and the client lack the support and legal protection of an employing institution or agency. This means that counsellors in private practice should be the most experienced of all counsellors. This is recognized by BAC in their Information Sheet 6, which offers guidance to those setting up in private practice. BAC states that 'appropriate competence and experience are basic prerequisites' and suggests that being a BAC accredited counsellor would be a minimum standard of competence necessary.

The accreditation scheme enables counsellors to be accredited through two different routes: either they fulfil specified training criteria or they will have had ten years' experience. Eligibility for accreditation under the 'training clause' means that a counsellor either has to have received a formal training by completing

a recognized course or to have received sufficient training in
counselling to form a 'core' and then attended other courses to
have accumulated a minimum of 250 hours of theory and 200
hours of skills training. It is also necessary to have had 450
hours of supervised counselling practice over a minimum period
of three years. To be eligible to be accredited under the 'ten
years' experience clause' an applicant has to have had 'a minimum of 150 hours per year practice under formal supervision'
for at least ten years. In addition, regardless of the route to
accreditation, counsellors have to:

1 Submit evidence of commitment to continued personal and
  professional development;
2 Give a description of their personal and theoretical counselling philosophy, showing how this is congruent with their
  work;
3 Present two 1000 word case-studies, one of which illustrates
  how supervision is integrated into counselling practice;
4 Prepare a diary of a month's counselling work, identifying the
  main concerns of each session;
5 Supply a supervisor's report and a reference.

All these submissions are assessed by a team of five Accredited
Counsellors who then make their recommendation to the BAC
accreditation sub-committee. For a counsellor to become accredited, at least three of the team have to recommend accreditation.

There is no doubt that anyone eligible for accreditation by
either of these routes should have the levels of experience and
skills necessary for independent practice. Unfortunately, many
counsellors setting up in the independent sector do not have these
qualifications. Indeed, at present there is nothing to stop anyone
with no training or qualifications from setting up in practice as a
counsellor. This lack of statutory regulation leaves the consumer/
client who is seeking counselling in the independent sector in a
vulnerable position with little or no protection against malpractice.

An awareness of the vulnerability of the general public resulted
in several articles in the press in 1991 and 1992. Two magazines,
Essentials and the Consumers' Association publication, *Which Way
to Health?*, and one newspaper, *The Independent*, have suggested
the sort of questions that should be asked of any counsellor
when 'shopping around' for counselling. The most detailed of

these is from the Consumers' Association and suggests four steps. These are:

1 *Decide what you want*
   - What do you want to get out of therapy – why are you seeking it, and what result would mean it had been successful?
   - Do you want long-term support or help with a short-term problem? How much can you afford?
   - What type of therapy would suit you?
2 *Find possible therapists*
   - A recommendation by a friend or GP is a good way to find a therapist.
   - Contact the British Association for Counselling. They can send a list of therapists in your area. Some are accredited by BAC ... However, most are not.
   - Contact therapy organisations to ask whether any of their members practise in your area.
3 *Choose a therapist*
   Contact a therapist and discuss the following points:
   - What qualifications do they have, and what was the training that led to the qualifications?
   - How many years have they been practising, and how many hours of experience have they acquired?
   - Are they members of any professional organisation?
4 *Don't be pressured*
   - Don't be afraid to rely on your gut feelings: if you don't like the therapist, or feel they aren't helping you, then stop. Therapy is for *your* benefit – you have no obligation to the therapist.
   - If at any stage you think the therapist is behaving improperly, discuss it with them, stop seeing the therapist, or report them to their professional organisation.

BAC also gives guidelines to anyone looking for a counsellor. *Finding a Counsellor* (BAC Information Sheet 5) covers many of the points detailed above from the Consumers' Association.

For any independent practitioner concerned with good practice the pre-counselling information described in the last chapter answers all these questions and should be freely available so that a prospective client does not even have to ask them.

MEDICAL BACK-UP

It is important when unsupported by an institute or agency to have ensured the availability of a medical and psychiatric consultancy. This may involve paying a retainer fee for these services. There are times when a client's behaviour is difficult to unravel without medical knowledge and a counsellor may need specialist information on the effects of drugs, for instance. This requirement is sufficiently important for the BAC to ask in the application forms for accreditation for details of access to a medical consultancy.

All clients will have a GP and some will be receiving psychiatric care. Obviously it is very important to work in co-operation with anyone giving a client medical treatment. When this is the case, counsellors should write to the GP or psychiatrist informing them that a patient of theirs is seeking counselling, and check that there is no reason why the medical treatment and counselling should not proceed at the same time. It is not helpful to a client if there is no agreement between the different 'carers'. Counsellors vary in their practice when it comes to a client's GP, if the client is not actually being treated. Some will not take on a client for counselling unless permission has been given for the GP to be informed, and the GP has indicated that there are no contra-indications to counselling, such as a history of violence (see Chapter 3). Others insist that the client informs the GP themselves before counselling can begin. An alternative procedure is to let the client decide whether the GP should be informed or not. Still others may vary their policy and only inform a GP should the need arise.

As with so many counsellor–client interactions, there are times when the way a client handles the relationship between a counsellor and a GP gives considerable insight into the unconscious world of the client:

> Rachel had been John's counsellor for ten months. He had originally been referred by his GP and was receiving medication for depression. He seemed to be becoming increasingly depressed and Rachel began to wonder whether John should consult his GP again. She discussed this with John, who agreed that he would return to his GP.
>
> Next day Rachel received a phone call from John's GP.

John had agreed that they should communicate with one another. To Rachel's surprise the GP said that he saw no signs of a deepening depression, and did not see any need for a change in medication. This led Rachel to realize that there was significance in John showing her a different side of himself. She remembered his account of his grandmother always expecting him to be cheerful, and that when he was a child John felt that he only received attention from his mother when he was miserable and ill. These were the two key-carers in his childhood. When Rachel wondered out loud whether there was any connection between the way John handled herself and the GP, it suddenly made sense to John that he was handling the GP and Rachel as if they were these two carers from his childhood.

This example also illustrates the importance of cooperation between professionals. It is not uncommon for two professionals to find they are in conflict about the care of a client. This is often generated by the client and could be a replica of parents who were unable to co-operate over child-care, or of a child who gained power by playing one parent off against another. It is important that professionals involved in the care of a client communicate, and make this clear to their mutual client when confidentiality is initially discussed.

TELEPHONE

A telephone is essential, since it is a very common and now-adays almost universal means of communication. No counsellor, regardless of their work-setting, should be without one. It may seem odd, therefore, to include the telephone in this chapter rather than the previous one. The reason is that the majority of counsellors in the independent sector have neither a receptionist nor colleagues to take messages. This means that clients will talk to the counsellor direct. This has to be planned in advance, so that the telephone can be used to maximum advantage. The telephone can be a great absorber of time.

Counsellors also have to make a decision about whether they are prepared to offer telephone counselling and if so the maximum time they are willing to spend on the telephone. It is wise to make these policy decisions before a client demands it.

It is much easier for counsellors and clients if a response is proactive rather than reactive.

Although not essential, it is much better if all counselling-related calls are taken on a separate line from household calls. There are two main reasons for this. First, if counsellors work from their own home then the client calls will both impinge upon and intrude into the lives of anyone else living there. This may mean teaching members of the household what to say. At times it is difficult for them not to get involved in conversations that they do not want, and should not have to have, with clients. Second, it is easy for a phone call to be unexpected, resulting in an inappropriate response from a counsellor to a client. Indeed, on occasions that may be exactly what a client wants. This is illustrated in the following vignette. The counsellor giving the account thought she could manage without a business phone when starting out in independent practice:

> The telephone rang. I picked up the phone and heard, 'Hallo, it's Sue.' The voice was familiar and the manner very friendly, but to which Sue was I talking? As I racked my brain I said, 'How are you?' 'Oh fine,' said Sue. 'When can I see you?' Only then did I realize that this Sue was one of my clients. I felt that my tone of voice and manner had been far too familiar for our counselling relationship. Of course, it gave me an insight into Sue's desire to have me as a friend, but how I wished I had had my counsellor 'hat' on when I had answered the phone.

The BAC leaflet on private practice suggests that an answerphone is desirable, particularly if a counsellor does not have a receptionist. This means that a counselling session is not interrupted by the phone ringing. However, an answerphone is also useful because it enables counsellors to choose when to respond to a call. It also means a client can leave a message without the frustration of the phone rarely being answered during the working day. However, it should be recognized that some people are frightened of answerphones, particularly when they first have to use them; and others dislike leaving messages on one, perhaps with good reason. These messages are sometimes much more intimidating than is meant. Therefore counsellors need to listen to their answerphone messages as objectively as possible to check the tone of their voice and the actual message.

Answerphone messages also need to be checked periodically, because they do fade as the tape becomes worn.

Choosing when to respond is extremely important. Without the answerphone an instant response is necessary, and at some points in a stressful day it can be hard to remember that a reasonable response might be, 'I can't give you an answer at the moment. I will ring you back later.' It is very difficult to try to deal with phone calls in the gaps between sessions. It is common for counsellors to timetable about 15 minutes between sessions, which is enough time to clear their mind between one client and the next, but not enough to respond to phone calls. Frequently these phone calls need to be understood as part of the counselling process and therefore need a carefully thought-out response. Even if a phone call is a request for information or an assessment session, a counsellor needs both forethought and time to ensure that all the points outlined in the previous chapter are covered. It is important, therefore, for counsellors to choose to make the return call when the time is convenient and when they are prepared.

The answerphone can have another use for clients, apart from the obvious one of leaving messages. In some instances clients who are feeling very dependent, regressed and insecure, use the answerphone like a 'security blanket', finding that simply hearing the counsellor's voice is reassuring. This function of the answerphone is always useful, but particularly during breaks in the counselling.

The client using the answerphone in this way costs the counsellor nothing in calls, and only takes the time involved in listening to the message and deciding how to respond. In many instances the use of the phone means that the counsellor's time is involved. Counsellors in independent practice have to make three decisions related to the use of the phone before counselling starts so they can be proactive rather than reactive. These are whether a client may phone at all; if they may, then in what circumstances; and whether to charge for the counsellor's time or not. Once these decisions are made, they then form part of the contract between the counsellor and client (see Chapter 3). The question of charging will be mentioned later in this chapter.

An obvious reason for a phone call is to change or confirm an arrangement and to inform the counsellor of illness. These calls are usually brief and are necessary. All other phone calls will be related to what is happening in the counselling relationship and therefore part of the counselling process. It is these calls that need to be planned for and talked about in the initial contracting (see Chapter 3). Sometimes these will be 'emergency calls' because the client does not believe that she or he will last to the next session, or even feels suicidal. Others will be related to the client feeling rejected or abandoned, and so wanting to have a session there and then and not feeling able to wait until the next meeting.

If a counsellor works with clients with early emotional damage and believes that the path to emotional health involves regression and dependency, then his or her style of work will encourage this to occur. In working this way there are certain obligations. One of these is to carry part of the responsibility for the client feeling more infant- or child-like and vulnerable. This type of work is not exclusive to counsellors in independent practice. The difference is, that in my experience when working for an institution, clients rarely telephoned between sessions for support, whereas when I started practising independently they did. This may be because if counsellors work from home the clients know that, and may have more fantasies about their counsellors' endless availability. With this knowledge it is better to be proactive and make clients aware before the counselling starts that they may feel very vulnerable at times in the therapy and want to telephone.

Practice varies at this point. Some counsellors and therapists only accept the business-type phone calls between sessions (Kopp 1977: 97) and if clients ring about anything else rapidly state that the material must come to the next session. Others make it clear that telephone calls should only be made in a real emergency. This leaves the question of the differing definitions of a real emergency. Another approach is to accept all calls but perhaps put a time limit on the length of the call and/or the time of day when they are acceptable. Others state that they do not run an emergency service so that if a client feels suicidal she or he should contact the local Samaritans group. If phone calls are an agreed part of the contract then it is useful to outline to a client when they may be used. The following is an example:

Counsellor: You have my phone number, but I would ask you to respect my need for free time. I will then

understand that if you ring it is either because
an arrangement needs to be made or because
you think you cannot manage until the next
session. In a way, speaking with me will be a
bit like me 'rocking the cradle'. I don't actually
like counselling on the phone so I would not
want to spend more than 15 minutes on it. It is
much better if we can look at what is happening
in the sessions rather than in this less personal
way.

There may be rare occasions when a counsellor will offer a
client the possibility of a telephone session at a prearranged
time. This will be a way of enabling an exceptionally regressed
or vulnerable client to last from one session to the next, particularly when there is no space for an extra session in the
week. The decision to offer this has to be made with care and
sensitivity. It could actually undermine a client, confirming a
hidden belief that he or she is unable to manage.

There are also times when counsellors may need to phone a
client to alter arrangements because of a sudden change in plans
without enough time to write. Where possible it is better to
write, because any unexpected phone call from a counsellor is
an invasion into the client's life. Obviously such changes should
be kept to a minimum, because any sudden alteration can reduce the feeling of containment for the client. None the less,
alterations in the arrangements will have to be made occasionally,
and then the consequences looked at in the next session.

LETTERS

There are a number of similarities between letters and telephone
calls. They are both used for communicating, and their use and
the consequences need to be made clear in the initial agreement
with clients. Again, counsellors need to make decisions about
the use and handling of letters before meeting any clients, so
that they can be proactive. Some letters from counsellors, such
as the letter following an assessment session, are simply business
letters. None the less it has to be remembered that they can become transitional objects for clients, particularly if hand-written,

so they need to be drafted with care. Letters from clients can also be related to business.

The letters that need particular decisions are those that come to counsellors between sessions. They arise for the same reason as phone calls: for some clients, at particular points in the counselling, it is too long to wait until the next session. Reading letters takes time and the sending of these letters is a continuation of the counselling session. The first decision for counsellors is whether they are prepared to accept letters, apart from business letters. If these are acceptable, what should be done with letters that arrive between sessions? Should they be read, replied to and a charge made for the time, or read and replied to and no charge made? Should they be read, but not replied to, and a charge made for the reading time? Should they be kept and read with the client at the next session? Are there times when it would help a client to write a letter? The handling of letters by counsellors varies enormously: no letters; letters and responses, free of charge; letters but no response, free of charge; letters only and reading time charged for; and so on. The differences are related to theoretical background and experience (Kopp 1977: 98). It often does not initially cross the mind of an inexperienced counsellor that the client is using counsellor time, and that the letters can become unmanageable if their function is not explored. This is illustrated in the following vignette:

> Peter had worked as a volunteer in a counselling service for some years before he felt sufficiently confident to accept a private referral. His first client, June, had recently left her husband and wanted a counsellor with whom she could express her almost overpowering feelings of rage and sadness. Gradually Peter found it harder and harder to finish sessions on time and he felt extremely mean to be pushing her out and angry that he had given away so much time. With the help of supervision he understood that June may have feelings of never having enough of anyone's time. He found that this was true, and June had had fantasies of moving in with him. Once this and her sorrow at this 24-hour-service not being available was in the open, Peter could again end sessions on time with ease.
>
> Suddenly letters started arriving. He had never discussed letters in the original agreement with June, nor with his

supervisor. The first letter made it clear that June was very depressed and at her wits' end. She asked if he would ring her that evening. Peter felt so worried about her that he thought he must ring. It was very hard to end the phone call and it did not seem that he had helped her at all. A second similar letter arrived after the next session, though in the session there had been no hint of June's desperation. Peter discussed the letters at his next supervision and began to see that these were also about June's desire to be with him all the time. He also realized that he needed to think about letters and discuss them with a client when making the initial contract. It was difficult for him to introduce a rule about letters with June at this late stage in the counselling.

Letters can help a very dependent client survive from one week to the next without an extra session, in a similar but less invasive way than a phone call. There is no doubt that clients sometimes 'carry on a conversation' with their counsellor long after a session has ended and it may help to clear their mind by writing. It is analogous to any other important life or business transaction which needs confirmation in writing. A common view is that if it is session material it should be charged for, otherwise clients could have guilty feelings about stealing the counsellor's time, though some clients will revel in getting that extra time. Other reasons for letters between sessions are that some clients think they are forgotten by the counsellor. Sometimes, all a client's negative feelings about the counsellor are expressed in letters and none appear in the session. Another use is to 'dump' unpleasant memories on to paper and then send them to the counsellor, as a way of clearing the client's mind of something unbearable. Clients can also be hungry/greedy for their counsellor's time and use letters to gain some extra time. Whatever a counsellor's practice in regard to when a letter is read, the unconscious feelings associated with letters need to be brought into the open in a session. Therefore the content and the feelings must be discussed and the client enabled to express them directly during sessions.

There are times when it may positively help a client if they are encouraged to write a letter. Again the rules have to be clear on how it is to be handled. For some clients their counsellor's

holiday break may be unbearably long, and without an institution to turn to for help, they may find writing a letter helpful.
Letter writing also can help clients who are discovering that
they have been severely sexually or physically abused, as the
following example shows:

> Christine had been coming for counselling for about eight
> months. Judith, her counsellor, had suspected for some
> time that Christine had been sexually abused when much
> younger. Gradually Christine was edging towards remem-
> bering this for herself. Towards the end of a session,
> Christine was suddenly beginning to recall the sexual abuse.
> It was as if her father was in the room and Christine was
> four years old. Judith was both 'there' with her client but
> also aware that she had to finish the session on time, and
> that there was no space to offer Judith an extra session if
> there was a lot of unfinished business. Of course, Judith
> knew that in some sense Christine had chosen the timing.
> Her 'gut' feeling was that her client needed to be both
> contained, so that ending on time was important, but that
> Judith would need to be especially available in a way
> Christine's family was not. Judith gently brought Christine
> back to the 'present day' and then said: 'I am aware that
> this has been a very important session today. It is possible
> that during this next week other memories will return.
> I cannot offer you an extra session this week but wonder
> whether it would help to write to me or ring me up.'
> Christine seemed surprised at this offer and checked that
> Judith really meant it. She then said: 'I don't know what
> will happen, but I will write, if I need to. It will help to
> think of these memories being held by you. It's safe here.'

There are occasions where I have offered to send a client a
postcard. It has happened that a client has become aware of a
needy child within him- or herself close to one of my holidays.
In making that decision I have known that the timing of this
will be significant in the unconscious world of the client, will
link to his or her lifestory, and that there is no institutional support. The following vignette is a description of such a situation:

> Jenny had been hospitalized for a week when she was one
> year old, and her mother had suffered from post-natal
> depression following the birth of her brother, when Jenny

was just two years old. For all her adult life she had been excessively independent and had never formed a committed relationship.

About six weeks before my two-week summer holiday, Jenny began to recognize how much she had come to depend on me. Whenever I encouraged her to think about what her feelings were about my holiday she changed the topic. I knew that this refusal to talk about the break was because she must be trying to pretend that it would not happen. When I brought this into the open, Jenny recalled that her parents had told her that they went on holiday without her just after she had been in hospital. She had been left with her aunt. The family story was that she had refused to eat until her mother returned. When I suggested that she thought they would never return and did not love her, she cried inconsolably. The misery of the one-year-old Jenny was palpable.

After discussion with my supervisor, and following a 'gut feeling' that Jenny needed to know tangibly that she was not forgotten, I suggested I send her a postcard. This I did. When I returned, Jenny admitted that she had not believed that I would send the card, but once I did she had carried it with her everywhere. In this first session after the break, Jenny began to understand that her response to her parents' absence when she was small was never to expect anything again. She also recognized how the card had been a sort of 'security blanket' for her. Touching it had reminded her that I existed.

FEES

Ferenczi (1928/1955: 92) commented that 'psycho-analysis is often reproached for being remarkably concerned with money matters'. The same could be said for any therapist or counsellor in independent practice. The main reason is that money has to change hands between clients and counsellors, which may result in it becoming the 'paramount dynamic in the therapy' (Temperley 1984). Temperley goes on to suggest that 'modern prudery is about money, and that resistance and transference now lodge as much in that taboo area as in sex'. Many counsellors are uneasy about charging fees, which Temperley suggests may be due to the projection of 'our needy, injured selves into our patients [sic], idealising both their need and our own meeting of their neediness'. When counsellors face their own financial needs, this can cause conflict which can force them into 'an healthy examination of the omnipotence and masochism which can underlie an undue identification with the underprivileged'. It is all too easy to forget that the apparent largesse in waiving a fee can be both patronizing and an abuse of power.

In the majority of cases clients pay their own fees. There are exceptions. A few health-insurance schemes will pay for a small number of sessions with a counsellor, provided this has been recommended in writing by a psychiatrist registered with the insurance company or by a GP. Parents do occasionally bring children, teenagers, or the whole family for counselling. Sometimes a client's employer/boss pays directly for counselling or indirectly through an EAP who employs the counsellor. In this case, care has to be taken not to collude with the client who may be unconsciously attacking his or her employer. One example of this collusion is that the client may refuse to terminate, where there is no fixed-term contract, perhaps as a way of punishing the employer. A way to avoid this problem is to clarify in the initial contract what is paid for by the employer and what is the client's responsibility. This is dealt with in more detail later in this chapter and in Chapter 5.

It is important to emphasize that work with families is very specialist and should not be undertaken without training. Late-teenagers may be suitable clients, but care has to be taken to establish whether the young adults have come for themselves rather than to placate an anxious parent. It may well be that young adults have no income of their own, they may not be at a Further Education or Higher Education Institute where counselling should be available, and there is no voluntary counselling service available to them. Counsellors may have to accept payment by the parents or refuse help to this age group. If these clients are accepted, then it will be important to work on dependency issues: a common enough problem with this age group.

Setting of fees

Clients need to know the fees for assessment sessions and counselling sessions (some counsellors charge less and others more for the former) and any rules associated with the fees before they enter a counselling relationship. A quick look at a BAC directory reveals enormous differences in the level of fees. Generally the fees are higher in the major cities and particularly in London and its environs. The range of fees for individual counselling in the 1993 BAC CPRD is from no charge to £80 per session. In London the median is £25 and in the rest of the UK £20. About 65 per cent of counsellors in the 1993 BAC CPRD give a range for their fee, or give a single fee stating that it is negotiable or there is a sliding scale. In London the lowest band is £5–£20, the two median ranges are £15–£25 and £20–£30, and the top band £40–£50. In the rest of the UK it is from £0–£12, to a median range of £15–£25 and the top band is £30–£60. A number of counsellors indicate that the final fee is related to income, in a few cases the fee for a session is stated to be £1 per £1,000 earned and in one case '1/20th of income' (though whether this is an annual fee is unclear). A few counsellors specify a lower fee for the unemployed or state that they have a few concessionary places, and some counsellors charge no fee in cases of hardship. Occasionally counselling is free, or a donation is asked for a charity, or it is left to clients to pay or not as they wish. Other variations on fee-setting are charging more for couples than individuals and for evening work than daytime. In the case of group work the fee for each member tends to be less than the fee for individual counselling, as might be expected.

Some of these enormous discrepancies can be explained because the setting of a fee will be related to personal and external factors. One personal factor is the value counsellors place on themselves and their training and skills; thus it is common for trainee counsellors to charge less. Another personal factor is an individual's philosophical and political ideologies, which might lead them to have a sliding scale or a negotiable fee, or make the decision that certain hardships warrant a reduced fee or even no fee. Other counsellors obviously do not want any income from their private counselling, either because they are in full-time employment or because they work for an agency such as MIND. They may charge no fee, though ask for a donation to a charity. This latter decision could be made because of a combination of a personal philosophy and the counsellor's theoretical training. Many counsellors believe that clients value themselves more when they give time and money to counselling. Thus there may also be valid therapeutic reasons for insisting on some payment, even if it is not for the benefit of the counsellor.

External forces also play their part in fee-setting. First and foremost, full-time counsellors have to determine how much they need to generate. This can only be decided once running costs are known. Counsellors working in London and its environs may well have higher overheads, so that fees tend to be higher. To some extent market forces will also affect what fees counsellors charge; thus experienced counsellors may charge more. Obviously the same revenue can be generated by charging fewer clients more, if the market will stand such an approach. It would rapidly become obvious if it will not.

The use of a sliding scale of fees to ensure that income is not a bar to counselling was mentioned in Chapter 3. This is another instance where the amount of income required will affect a counsellor's decision. Full-time counsellors will have to generate enough money at least to cover their overheads or they will be bankrupt. Obviously they cannot afford for all their clients to pay the lowest fee. This may be at least one reason why in some instances the range of the band is only £5. Where the band is very wide, with a range of as much as £45, this may be to try and ensure that the low fees are compensated for by the high fees.

A sliding scale may seem a reasonable way to offer counselling to a wider range of people, but often considerable negotiation will have to take place at the stage of making the contract. The counsellor must have criteria to operate the sliding scale, such as: the income of the client, whether gross or net income is used and, if the latter, is it the income left after tax or having taken into account certain fixed household expenses (e.g. mortgage/rent), and what constitutes hardship? It is important to realize that even the negotiation of the fee may affect the subsequent counselling. A way of reducing negotiation is to have a set number of concessionary places with clear, published criteria for eligibility. A good example of the negotiation of the fee affecting the therapeutic process is given by Maxine Anderson (1992). She describes how she took a patient [sic] on a low fee scheme, accepting the documentation to justify this. They negotiated that the fee would be increased as 'circumstances allowed'. Later in the therapy it became clear that the patient was shocked that her therapist had not bartered with her and had given in to her demands so easily; as a result she held the therapist in some contempt and the work in great disdain. Any attempts by the therapist to suggest that the low fee made her feel like a second-class patient were denied, and any reconsideration of the fee avoided. In her analysis of the transference, Anderson suggests that the patient 'felt herself to be very small' and the therapist 'to be the powerful adult who had the final say about items such as fees. In the face of this painful polarised position, the defence she resorted to was to curl up into a "tiny child, low fee status, no questions asked" posture which was not to be looked at nor thought about.'

The question of fees was one of a small number of practical recommendations Freud made to physicians when beginning the treatment of patients using the technique of psycho-analysis (1913/1958). He stressed that the fee 'must be decided at the beginning of the treatment' and that it does not help the patient if psycho-analysts charge a low fee or even no fee. He suggested that in so doing analysts are not acknowledging their 'actual claims and needs' and then affect their patients by feeling 'secretly aggrieved'. He makes the additional point that he experimented with 'gratuitous treatments' in the belief that this would result in as little resistance as possible to treatment. Instead he found it took longer, raising resistances in young men related to an 'opposition to an obligation to feel grateful' which hindered their acceptance of help. The absence of 'the regulating effect offered by the payment of a fee' removed a 'strong motive for endeavouring to bring the treatment to an end'. These problems of expected gratitude for a gift are as likely to occur with women as with men. This is another reason why counsellors need to give considerable thought to the fee structure that they set up, particularly when contemplating a sliding scale. The decision, after thought, may still be to offer some free or low fee places. If so, there again will be consequences, which may well appear in the transference material.

The following factors need to be taken into account when setting fees:

1 Overheads: cost of personal supervision, training and counselling/psychotherapy; travel to supervision, personal counselling, conferences and training sessions; telephone; postage and

stationery; advertising and pre-counselling leaflet; secretarial services; insurance; provision of personal pension; repairs; running costs of premises (heating, lighting, water, cleaning); sundries (paper handkerchiefs and lavatory paper); subscription to professional association(s); cost of professional journals and books; and possibly rental or mortgage of premises and council tax.

Where a private home is used then the cost of heating, light, repairs, household insurance water and cleaning, etc., will have to be calculated as a percentage of the cost for the whole house.

In my practice, single-handed, using rooms in my private house, these overheads have varied between £6,300 and £15,500 in the past four years. This variation has occurred because of engaging secretarial/reception assistance and the introduction of capital equipment (fax, answerphone, word-processor).

2 Generation of fees: when calculating the revenue from clients it is reasonable to assume that the working year is 40 weeks. This allows for holidays of counsellor and client, which may not coincide, and sessions cancelled by the counsellor because of other commitments such as a training day to further professional development, or minor indispositions.

It is clear from these considerations that many counsellors are not charging sufficient fees for counselling to be their full-time professional employment. A fee of £5 per session would generate £7,800 a year, and this assumes that six people are being seen each weekday and for 52 weeks of the year. This level of work would be irresponsible to both counsellor and client, if not impossible. There will be several reasons for these low fees. First, additional revenue may be generated by such activities as running training courses, and supervising other counsellors. Second, some counsellors charge lower-than-average fees because they are in full-time employment, often as a counsellor, and so only see two or three private clients a week in their spare-time; therefore they do not rely on their private work to create a viable income. A third reason may be that a number of people enter counselling having trained and worked in a voluntary agency. It is unlikely that they have actually costed counselling, because they are not working independently to create their sole source of finance. This lack of a fee structure, which reflects the fact that counselling is not a registered profession, is of considerable concern because it undermines the full-time professional counsellor in independent practice. This will be discussed further in Chapter 6.

Payment of fees

Once the fee is set and agreed, there is the question of the method of payment. Fees can be paid in advance or arrears, in cash or by cheque, and the frequency of payment will vary: weekly or monthly are common arrangements. Freud (1913/ 1958: 131) cautioned against allowing 'large sums of money to accumulate' and 'to ask for payment at fairly short intervals – monthly, perhaps'. However, letting the client make these decisions can again give the counsellor insight into the internal world of the client. The majority of clients choose to pay at the end of a session if paying weekly and in arrears if paying monthly. It is therefore noticeable and worth exploration when the occasional client pays in advance:

> Janet was the eldest in a large family. There were always babies in the house, who needed feeding or their nappies changed. Janet often helped her mother, that was one way of spending time with her, but it was very rare for her to spend time alone with her mother.
>
> As a client Janet was always punctual and kept all her negative feelings about her counsellor, Mike, hidden. She insisted on paying once a month in advance, and would make out the cheque in front of Mike at the start of the first session of the month. Having observed this for some time, Mike began to think that both paying in advance and losing some session time once a month must have a meaning. If Janet could understand the meaning it might enable her to express her feelings more freely.
>
> Mike drew Janet's attention to the way she paid him, suggesting it had a special meaning. Perhaps it was related to her uncertainty about her mother having time for her. Was buying the time in advance a way of ensuring that Mike had to give her time? This seemed to make sense to Janet and was followed by a string of memories about how

busy her mother was. Janet's response confirmed for Mike that she had begun to understand the payment in advance.

The manner in which payment is made also reveals much about a client's feelings towards a counsellor. It is not difficult to detect anger when a cheque is flung on to a table. More hidden at the time of payment is the anger, only revealed later, when a cheque 'bounces', is unsigned, undated or made out for too little. From a business point of view, perhaps counsellors should insist that cheque-card numbers are put on the backs of cheques and let clients find other covert ways of expressing negative feelings – they will find them!

Changing the fees

If a counselling relationship with a client lasts more than a year, it is likely that fees will have to be raised, at least in line with the cost of any inflation. It will have been in the initial contract that a counsellor will inform a client of a fee increase. It would be reasonable to give at least a month's notice of such a change. Needless to say, such a change will bring every type of reaction; from nothing, to mute resignation, to reasonableness, to down-right fury. This is another example of how much unconscious material can come to the surface when something changes in the counselling relationship.

It is not only the client who responds to unconscious forces: counsellors do as well. Temperley (1984) gives a good example. She became aware when reviewing fees that one patient [sic] 'was paying £2 less than others in a similar financial situation'. There was a rational reason related to when the patient began therapy but Temperley was aware of her reluctance to raise the matter. As she reflected on the reason for this, Temperley recalled that this patient had had a placating mother, and the patient had 'felt hamstrung by the mother's inability to be forthrightly aggressive'. This led the therapist to suspect that her 'tardiness about raising her fee' indicated that she was 'caught up in re-producing her [patient's] mother's masochism', and maintaining the patient's 'unconscious sense of [her] as someone placating like her mother'. It is important to review what clients are paying. I have found it surprising to see how often a client has become a 'special case' without any conscious transaction between them and me. When this occurs it is important for counsellors to identify and explore the reasons for this, both in terms of themselves and their clients. For the counsellor these might be fear of the client's anger and rage, or feeling an 'ogre' or a soft touch or feeling sorry for the client. All of these counter-transference feelings are useful material for understanding more about the client and need to be brought into the open and understood.

There are times when raising the fee can cause genuine hardship and the client's circumstances do change so he or she has greater difficulty in paying the fee. Decisions then have to be made about whether to hold the fee at its original level in the first case and to lower them in the second. Counsellors have to follow their intuitive sense of the truth of the situation in deciding what to do. There is no doubt that genuine financial problems can suddenly happen. Whatever decision is made it is certain there will be consequences which will be detectable in a change in the dynamics of the counselling relationship. In writing of how the transactions around fees can become 'the paramount dynamic in the therapy', Temperley (1984) comments that 'many beginner therapists hesitate to interpret' this dynamic 'because it is lodged in the form of money'. This is just as true of experienced counsellors, and not just beginners.

Rules about fees

Other decisions have to be made in the agreement about fees, relating to missed appointments, cancellations and holidays. Counsellors in independent practice vary enormously in the way they handle these issues. At one end of the spectrum a client pays for all the appointments they miss or cancel and for holiday absences unless they coincide with the counsellor's. At the other end of the spectrum, no charge is made in any of these circumstances. In between, many counsellors charge for a missed session unless they are given sufficient notice of cancellation; they do not charge for missed sessions when a client's holiday does not coincide with theirs, again provided there is sufficient notice. Sufficient notice for a cancellation might be three days, though it is rare to be able to offer an appointment to someone else within this time; perhaps a week is more realistic. Sufficient notice of a holiday might be at least a month in advance.

Different counsellors will have their own theoretical and

pragmatic reasons for such decisions. The fundamental difference hinges on the attitude of the counsellor to the session.
Freud's view was that the client was leasing a definite hour of
his time each day (1913/1958: 126). It therefore belongs to the
patient, and 'he [sic] is liable for it even if he does not make use
of it'. Freud then went on to discuss the effects of a 'less stringent'
approach to sessions. He commented that the result was that
'the "occasional" non-attendances increase so greatly that the
doctor finds his material existence threatened; whereas when
the arrangement is adhered to, it turns out that accidental
hindrances do not occur at all and intercurrent illnesses only
occasionally . . . Nothing brings home to one so strongly . . . the
non-existence of chance, as a few years' practice of psychoanalysis on the strict principle of leasing by the hour.' A consequence of this approach is that a counsellor will always charge
when a client cancels because of illness. This is done in the belief
that falling ill is not a chance event, that it occurs at a particular
point in counselling and the client's life for a reason. Thus it is
an integral part of the therapy and needs to be interpreted.
Clients who know they will be charged can be ill and cancel a
session knowing that their non-attendance does not affect their
counsellor financially. This removes a potential source of guilt.

Some therapists carry this attitude to sessions a step further
than Freud. He was prepared to break off treatment if a patient
developed 'undoubted organic illnesses', and felt entitled 'to
dispose elsewhere of the hour which becomes free, and take the
patient back again as soon as he [sic] has recovered' and Freud
had another hour vacant (Freud 1913/1958: 127). It is not clear
from this paper how long the patient was ill, but for some counsellors and therapists it is not acceptable to give a client's session
to someone else. In doing so the counsellor is neither valuing
the regularity nor the continuity of counselling nor recognizing
the special place that therapy has for the client. An analogy is
made between the counselling hour and the regular breast- or
bottle-feeding that the small baby receives. The milk belongs to
the baby and is not given to anyone else. If it is, this will rightly
evoke anger and envy. With this approach to the counselling
relationship, while cancellation is sometimes unavoidable, non-
payment for the session is never acceptable, because offering the
session to someone else is unacceptable and thus is not an option.
There will come a point, which has to be negotiated with the
client, when it is no longer realistic to apply this rule. It cannot

be applied if the illness is long-term. It is important that the decision is tempered by common sense.

The pragmatic reason for charging is that if clients do not attend a session, which has been agreed and reserved for them, and cannot be assigned to anyone else, then a counsellor's weekly revenue is reduced. At a business level the self-employed must generate enough to cover their costs. Other counsellors, who make no charge when clients cancel through illness, take a different view. This is that it is unfortunate to be ill, that the client cannot help this, and it should not be exploited. Indeed, it may be thought unreasonable and even punitive to charge in these circumstances. However, the counsellor with this approach could be in a precarious financial situation in a major flu epidemic!

Where cancellation is due to a work commitment there is a similar variety of responses, reflecting a similar range of attitudes, from charging for the session because it belongs to the client, or believing it is unreasonable to penalize someone for their employer's demands.

Many counsellors start out in independent practice charging no fee for cancellation and gradually move to the middle of the spectrum, charging for missed sessions but making a distinction between cancellations on the grounds of illness and those made for other reasons. The latter are charged for unless there has been an agreed amount of notice. Illness is usually much less predictable and therefore it is not realistic to insist on a week's notice. Therefore these cancelled sessions are not charged for, nor is 'sufficient notice' required.

Independent practice gives a counsellor a different view of missed and cancelled sessions from those directly employed by agencies or institutions. Indeed, the latter could learn from the former. If a client misses a session and a counsellor decides, 'perhaps masochistically' (Temperley 1984), not to charge, it hurts the counsellor's pocket. Whereas employed counsellors can more easily ignore the meaning of a missed session, because the employer absorbs the cost. As a result, there may be collusion between the client and the counsellor which could mirror the collusion between the 'child and mother to evade how the child is mocking the father and his rights' (Temperley 1984).

Clients also need guidance about fees when a session overruns. The need for containment means that this should be an unusual event. There are times when a counsellor will decide that a little extra time may help a client. This should be offered and not 'just happen', and it should be clear on what basis this time is given and can be taken. The extra time may be negotiated on a pro rata basis or it may be free. Occasionally it has seemed inappropriate to interrupt a session with a comment about time. In these instances, if I have made the decision to overrun without consulting my client, then I do not charge for the time. It was my decision and I carry the responsibility for it.

A further decision related to fees is the cost of using the phone for counselling, and the cost of letters being read. This is another area on which counsellors in private practice vary. Some charge the standard counselling fee on a pro rata basis, others do not charge. It only takes one client to abuse the use of the phone or the sending of letters to make a counsellor review policy. Whatever the policy, clients need to know what it is at the time of the original agreement.

BALANCE OF WORK

I have already noted that counsellors in the independent sector are free to make their own decisions about the balance of short-term to long-term work in their case load. It is common for independent counsellors to have many more long-term than short-term clients. One reason is the counsellor's personal preference, and another reason, sufficient demand from clients to allow this. This may be a result of the NHS, counselling services and EAPs which often restrict counselling and psychotherapy to relatively short-term work. Another reason may be that clients with considerable dependency needs may unconsciously seek out counsellors in the independent sector working from home. The home environment may fulfil part of a fantasy of being a child again in the family home. The responsibility counsellors bear if they undertake such long-term work has already been mentioned in terms of the additional support that may need to be supplied.

HOLIDAYS

The difficulty of the lack of institutional support and the effect of its absence on vulnerable clients when counsellors are on holiday has already been mentioned, as has the use of the telephone and letters to enable some vulnerable clients to manage in holiday breaks. However, even these supports may not be enough for the most vulnerable. Another support is to ask another counsellor if he or she would be prepared for a client to be able to make contact by phone and to offer a session if necessary. A counsellor's supervisor might be a suitable person, because he or she will know something of the client's difficulties. This type of agreement is rather like a child going to a grandparent while a parent is on holiday. Needless to say, it will affect subsequent counselling when the original counsellor returns. The replacement counsellor could be experienced by the client as being much better than the original counsellor, or no use at all. This could be true, for some counsellors are better than others. Alternatively, either reaction could have its origins in the early experience of the client and as such can be useful in understanding the client. Feedback from vulnerable clients is that it is comforting to have an alternative counsellor available, whether or not contact is made.

Considerably less vulnerable clients may also find the prospect of a counsellor being on holiday for two to three weeks daunting. A small object from the counselling room, such as a polished or varnished pebble, a shell or a dried flower, is often sufficient to remind them of the relationship and thus brings comfort. It has to be made clear whether the object is on loan or may be kept. Of course, to be able to offer this a counsellor needs to have such objects in the counselling-room, perhaps in a bowl.

SAFETY

In discussing advertising and assessment it has been emphasized that a counsellor must be concerned for their own safety. Particularly when working alone, both the counsellor and client are vulnerable to sexual harassment or attack and violence. Some measures were mentioned briefly in Chapter 3: in particular, never seeing a new client without a 'chaperone' in the building, checking a client's history with a GP, and having an alarm. While no personal alarm will protect someone from attack, the principle is that the loud noise will frighten off all but the most determined. A personal alarm can be bought and kept in a pocket, or attached to a belt, so it is available instantly should the need arise. A number of companies specializing in burglar alarms (security systems) supply either a fixed panic button, or an alarm small enough to be held. When these are activated, they set off the burglar alarm. Obviously, the personal alarm is more versatile than a fixed panic button, in particular because the former can be taken from room to room and to the front door, and because the latter has to be attached discreetly to a piece of furniture, a door lintel or windowsill. In all these instances, counsellors will have to move from their chair to set them off, which may disturb the violent person more and lose precious seconds.

The evidence from surveys in Great Britain and the US suggests that clients are more vulnerable to sexual abuse than any other professional misconduct. The majority of complaints received by BAC are of accusations by clients of sexual abuse by counsellors. Probably about 10 per cent of practising counsellors sexually abuse their clients. A client's only safeguard, as mentioned earlier, is to ensure that a counsellor belongs to a professional organization such as BAC, with a Code of Ethics and Practice and a complaints procedure. At least this means the client has some route of redress, although until there is a compulsory National Register and counsellors are chartered the counsellor can continue to practise (see Chapter 6).

MOVING HOUSE

The ending of a counselling relationship because a counsellor moves house to another town or city was mentioned in Chapter 3. It can happen that a counsellor moves house or counselling rooms within their own city and the clients move as well. Clients should be given as much notice as possible, and if possible where a sale is taking place, before a 'For Sale' board goes up. For some clients the inevitability of the situation will evoke unconscious material about similar occasions in their own past. Children are often not consulted about a move; it is inevitable and happens whether they like it or not and the resulting losses are frequently not sufficiently acknowledged. Even if clients did not move house as children they will have experienced other transitions. For instance, moving to a senior school is generally inevitable and can involve loss and disruption. The following is an example of the effects of a counsellor moving:

> Fred decided to move his counselling room from his private house to an office block. He gave all his clients two months' notice. Christopher was obviously very angry about the impending move, saying he would rather end than move; it would never be the same again. Fred's move reminded him that when he was four years old his parents had split up, and he and his mother had moved to live with his grandparents. He had been very frightened of his grandfather and there had been no children close by to play with. As he began to understand the associations he seemed to be less angry; but there was more to come. On the last session in Fred's house, Christopher ran over a flower-bed with his car. When he arrived for the first session at the new office, he arrived very late saying that 'he had got lost'. He brought with him a pot-plant for Fred's new office. The plant was a creeping fig. The name gave Fred an uncomfortable feeling; he also feared that the plant would not survive as he did not like house-plants.

Moving house is a stressful time for anyone. A counsellor will have to cope with this and also the effects of the move on their clients. If the move involves a counsellor's family, then their envy may be heightened, knowing that clients are given a haven of calm and order compared with the rest of the house. This may make yet further demands on the counsellor. Therefore it may be necessary to have extra support from a supervisor at this time.

INSURANCE AND PENSION ARRANGEMENTS

The BAC Code of Ethics and Practice for Counsellors specifies that 'counsellors should take all reasonable steps to ensure that the client suffers neither physical nor psychological harm during counselling' (B2.2.1). This means counsellors must prepare themselves very thoroughly before ever seeing a client. In practical terms every precaution must be taken to ensure that clients do not hurt themselves while on a counsellor's premises. It is important for a counsellor to look round their premises with an eye for possible hazards and to remove them where possible. Obviously it is impossible to ensure that accidents never occur and so insurance must be taken out. A client who is hurt can seek compensation. It is unlikely that a Household Insurance Policy will cover parts of premises used for business purposes, so counsellors working from home must check whether they need Public Liability Insurance. Without this, counsellors might find themselves liable for damages (Bond, forthcoming). If counsellors work in business premises, public liability cover should exist, but it is important to check that this is displayed and that there is sufficient cover, or counsellors can find themselves having to meet all or part of the claim (Bond, forthcoming). Offices must also comply with the Fire Regulations and the Health and Safety at Work Act.

The duty to take all reasonable steps not to cause psychological harm is much more onerous. A counsellor, in common with every professional, is required 'to exercise reasonable care and skill in rendering services to clients' (Bond, forthcoming). The difficulty is establishing what this means for a counsellor. Bond's research has established that the courts do not assess effectiveness as a criterion for reasonable care, but rather look at what is accepted practice. If a counsellor acts in ways accepted by 'a reasonable body of competent professional opinion' then they cannot be judged as negligent. This issue is explored and examined in some depth by Bond. A counsellor in independent practice needs to have a Professional Indemnity Policy to cover them against a claim for malpractice, errors or omissions.

Bond also recommends that any insurance pack should also include Libel and Slander Insurance and Product Insurance. The former is necessary, because the work of a counsellor does make charges of defamation possible; the latter is necessary where counsellors produce such items as stress-reduction tapes. Details of some insurance brokers who have specialized in insurance packages for counsellors are given in Appendix D.

Counsellors will have to consider whether they need to buy insurance to cover loss of earnings owing to ill-health. If they make Class 2 National Insurance contributions they will be entitled to self-certificated sickness benefit, but this is likely to be considerably less than normal earnings. It is extremely expensive to buy insurance cover for short-term illness, but cover in the event of a permanent disability or chronic illness which prevents any earning is less expensive. Counsellors need to seek expert advice on this type of insurance. It is not allowable as a business expense.

Expert advice also needs to be sought on making provision for retirement by arranging a personal pension or a 'money purchase' scheme. There are Inland Revenue rules about what percentage of taxable income may be spent on such premiums.

ACCOUNTS AND TAXATION

It is always wise to consult a professional accountant when first starting to be self-employed, because legislation and taxation is liable to change. The Inland Revenue publish a number of free leaflets which are helpful and offer guidance to anyone setting up in business. The four most useful ones are: *Starting in Business* (IR 28), *Simple Tax Accounts* (IR 104), *How Your Profits are Taxed* (IR 105), and *Capital Allowances for Vehicles and Machinery* (IR 106). A business can be full-time, part-time or spare-time, which covers any counsellor earning money from self-employed counselling work.

As soon as counsellors start in independent practice they should inform both their local Tax Office and, if they are not employed elsewhere, the Department of Social Security to arrange National Insurance contributions. In addition, if taxable turnover exceeds limits set by the Inland Revenue, counsellors must register for VAT. The local VAT office, whose address will be found in the telephone directory under 'Customs and Excise', will give the current limit. This latter registration is unlikely, unless other work is being done within the practice, such as training. Only four people in the 1990 BAC CPRD and one person in the 1993 directory indicated that they were registered for VAT. While not essential, it is often easier to open a separate bank account for the practice. It is essential, however, to keep accurate records and accounts from the start. This means keeping records of all money received from clients, although it is not necessary to give them receipts unless requested. Records should also be kept of all expenditure associated with the practice, retaining receipts as far as possible. It helps to list these receipts, totalling them monthly, and to give each one a number for cross-referencing with the account book. The Tax Inspector has the right to disallow any expense not properly vouched for. It is good practice to have a notebook in which entries are made of all journeys undertaken associated with the business and of all other relevant expenses (postage, telephone calls, etc.). A further decision to be made is the choice of accounting date. This then becomes the annual date for making up accounts, which must be kept. The date chosen is often the end of the first year's trading, but it does not have to be. It is perhaps easier to make that date the end of a month. Alternatives are the end of the calendar year on 31 December, or the end of the tax year on 5 April.

If a firm of accountants is employed, they will draw up the business accounts, though the responsibility for the accuracy of these always remains with the person signing the tax return. This is another reason why it is good practice to keep accounts, whether an accountant assists or not. First, this ensures that the counsellor employing the accountant knows the information is accurate and can be easily checked. Second, this will reduce the accountant's fees. A wide variety of account books can be bought from office-stationery suppliers. For annual summary and monthly accounts, a petty cash daybook with ruled columns for analysis is adequate. Commercially, books are available with standard column rulings and an inspection of the inside cover of any analysis cashbook will give an indication of this. There should be one to suit every need. I have found an A4 book with one 'dr' (debit) column and eleven 'cr' (credit) columns of analysis quite adequate (1dr. 11cr.), though I use it in reverse, with expenditure analysed in the eleven columns and using the single column for receipts (see Appendix E). This analysis enables separate items of expenditure to be identified. For counsellors these separate items are costs of supervision and personal counselling or psychotherapy; postage; telephone; stationery, books and photocopying; training and conference fees; travel and subsistence; advertising; secretarial; insurances; and repairs and sundries.

'Secretarial' may entail employing someone, full- or part-time, and this opens a whole new area concerning employment and the liability for deducting Income Tax and National Insurance contributions and paying them to the Collector of Taxes. This is another area where advice will be required. A leaflet entitled *Thinking of Taking Someone On?* (IR 53) is available from the local Tax Office and is essential reading if a counsellor is intending to become an employer.

A small number of transactions in any year may be made on items which are classed as capital items: examples are an answerphone, a fax, a word-processor and a bank loan. I include these in the 'sundries' column and categorize them at the end of the year. Again, each individual may need to take professional advice on how to handle this.

By law a 'true return of income', which includes business profits, has to be made each year. The amount which is taxable is after expenses have been deducted and has to be agreed with the Inspector. Depending on the turnover before expenses, the return can either be summary or full business accounts. Advice will also need to be taken on this, because the limit of gross business turnover below which a simple summary is acceptable to the Tax Office is set each year by the Chancellor of the Exchequer in the Finance Bill and will change. Once the accounts have been received for the first year of business, the Tax Inspector determines the tax payable and then sends an assessment. The arrangements for paying tax by the self-employed has changed as a result of the 1993 Finance Bill, following the Spring Budget. As the implications of this are not clear at the time of writing, advice will have to be sought. Whatever changes take place it is important to put some money on one side, otherwise the tax for more than one year will have to come out of current income. The Tax Office also calculates and collects earnings-related Class 4 National Insurance contributions.

When self-employed, counsellors should be paying Class 2 contributions once their income rises above a figure, which needs to be ascertained. It is set annually by the Chancellor in the Budget. These contributions are paid quarterly and are collected by the Department of Social Security. They can be paid by direct debit from a bank account or by stamps on a card. Generally speaking, the direct debit method is easier. Provided a person's contribution record fulfils certain criteria, they are entitled to claim sickness benefit when ill. These contributions also go towards the Basic State Retirement Pension. Anybody thinking of becoming self-employed would be well-advised to obtain a pension forecast from the Department of Social Security, who will provide a form for this on request. This will help individuals make decisions on whether to pay Class 3 contributions to fill gaps in their contribution records, or whether to make their own private arrangements. The following leaflets published by the Department of Social Security are relevant: *National Insurance Contributions Class 2 + 4 for Self-employed People* (Leaflet NP 18) and *National Insurance Contributions for People with Small Earnings from Self-employment* (Leaflet NI 27A).

The situation is considerably more complicated where a counselling partnership is formed. There are legal implications and more onerous financial responsibilities, owing to the joint liability. It is important to consult both a solicitor and an accountant before entering into such an agreement with others. To some counsellors this area of accounting and taxation may be somewhat worrying. The simple maxim is, 'if in doubt, ask'.

If any counselling practice is wound up, again an accountant may be helpful. In any case the Tax Office must be informed of the date on which it will end, and whether the practice is ending because of retirement or changed type of employment. As soon as possible, accounts must be prepared covering the time from when accounts were last prepared up to the date on which the practice ended.

SATISFACTIONS AND STRESSES

All counselling work has its satisfactions and stresses, some of which will be in common, regardless of the work-setting. The major reasons for choosing to work in independent practice were mentioned in Chapter 2. As is always the case, each decision carries with it consequences, some of which are stressful. For instance, the stress of working in a group can be disagreements among the group members. One stress of working alone in the private sector can be isolation, unless this is counteracted by deliberately making time to meet other counsellors. Many counsellors choose independent practice because it gives them autonomy, and removes the interference of an employer, but a major stress of being self-employed, particularly at the start, is surviving financially (Feltham 1992). Feltham also comments on how the increased professionalization of counselling, with a requirement for on-going supervision and professional development, has brought further demands on limited financial resources.

Limited financial resources also may mean that a counsellor in the independent sector cannot afford to be a member of any major professional committees. Attending any weekday meeting may involve loss of earnings, which might not be affordable at the start of being self-employed. Once an independent practice is established, the decision to join any professional committee will be made in the knowledge that this could affect earnings. At the moment, though this may well change, employers tolerate and even encourage their employee counsellors to belong to such committees. It would be unfortunate if all the major decisions about counselling practice made by BAC and BPS were made by counsellors in employment, particularly when there are a significant number of counsellors in the independent sector. The professional committees themselves must begin to recognize this and accommodate independent practitioners in an acceptable way.

Another consequence of joining any professional committees is that client sessions may have to be cancelled to fit in with the committee schedule. Not all committees have meetings on the same day of the week and at the same time. This means that clients miss sessions some weeks either because a counsellor cannot offer an alternative time that week or because the time offered does not suit the client. For some counsellors it is unacceptable to be unable to offer the containment of regular sessions, week in and week out: in which case they cannot do this type of committee work. Others make it clear in the original contract (see Chapter 3) that there will be missed sessions because of external commitments. As with all other areas of the work, the agreements and arrangements must be clear.

Counselling in an institution has advantages that have already been mentioned in several chapters. However, there are stresses in an institution, such as the marginalization of the counselling service and the competition with all the other departments for limited resources. In the independent sector, not surprisingly, marginalization and competition also arise, although the reasons are different. The next chapter looks at these stresses and their origins, and the relations between counsellors in independent practice and other workers.

· FIVE ·

Professional relationships in counselling in independent practice

One of the dangers of independent practice, particularly if working alone, is isolation. But, of course, there are other workers who do or can impinge on a self-employed counsellor. There is no need to be isolated and indeed, as I mentioned in Chapter 3, counsellors have a responsibility to 'look after' themselves, and one way of doing this is by forming networks with colleagues. This chapter will focus on relationships with peers, referring agencies, other professionals, training institutes and others who might consider using the skills of counsellors in the independent sector to train their employees, and with the training bodies within the profession.

PEERS

The relationship between counsellors in any one area of the country is highly complex. Peers may be friends; colleagues forming a support network; the source of referrals; the recipients of referrals; the source of counsellors/therapists, supervisors, and trainers; rivals and also competitors. While some of the activities listed are compatible, others are not. For instance, it is in breach of the BAC Code of Ethics and Practice for Trainers for a trainer to have a client as trainee. The more isolated the area and the smaller the number of counsellors in it, the more difficult it is to keep these boundaries sacrosanct, and the more likely it is that counsellors will not be able to adhere rigidly to these standards of good practice.

It has been mentioned that part of 'taking care of yourself' is to form a network of support. This might involve meeting other counsellors on a regular basis. One forum could be a local counselling group. However, it would be very likely for a counsellor to find that, for instance, the guest speaker was already known to them, perhaps being someone who had trained them. They might also encounter some of the following: friends, past clients, present clients, supervisors, personal counsellors/therapists, their psychotherapist/counsellor executors, and their trainers. Whereas some analytic and psychodynamic groups have a code of practice forbidding meetings where such encounters take place, such a strict rule applied anywhere but London at present would be both unrealistic and impractical. Therefore a convention has developed that where there is a 'boundary' that must be maintained, both parties are simply courteous to one another and do not enter into conversation.

Another difficulty relating to boundaries is if counsellors wish to take an active part in the committee of a local counsellors' group. Again, they could find that they are working with people who have been, or are, clients, trainees or supervisees. Similarly, the counsellor could have been or is a client, trainee or supervisee of someone already on the committee. If a counselling relationship is in process, the counsellor should withdraw rather than the client, assuming the client was there first. If it is the other way round, then the counsellor should discuss the situation with the client and explore together why she or he joined. This may reveal transference material that gives insight into the client's unconscious world. It will certainly have consequences in the counselling process if the counsellor insists that it is inappropriate for a client to be on the same committee, and the client should stand down. The following vignette illustrates this point:

A local counselling group had both practising counsellors and people interested in counselling as members. Tim, a counsellor, was on the executive committee. He knew that Jacky, his client, who was training as a counsellor, was a member of the group, but they rarely attended the same meetings. Should they do so, Jacky always told him in advance that she was attending, and kept 'a low profile'.
At a meeting of the executive Tim was surprised to hear that Jacky had accepted the suggestion of the Chair that she should be co-opted to the committee. He first felt very puzzled that Jacky had not told him about this, and then

angry. At the next session she still said nothing so he decided
that he must say something to her. He said, 'Jacky, I was
at the Counselling Group executive meeting last week and
I gather you are joining the group as a co-opted member.'
'Oh yes,' said Jacky. 'I'm very pleased.' Tim said, 'I imagine
you must have wondered how it would affect our counselling relationship.' 'Mmm, I didn't think it would matter.
You see me at meetings anyway.' When Tim suggested
that attending an occasional meeting was different from
working on the same executive committee, Jacky was
annoyed and accused Tim of being very controlling. She was
just as angry when the session ended.

In the next session, they unravelled why Jacky had felt
so angry. She felt pleased and 'grown-up' to be asked and
had never considered saying 'no'. When Tim had presumed,
incorrectly, that she had considered all the implications,
she had felt silly and 'small'. This reminded her of earlier
feelings. Her parents wanted her to be 'grown-up' but did
not tell her when her Gran had died. When she eventually
discovered this, her parents said they had not told her
because she was too young. She recognized that joining
the executive committee was an attempt to be 'grown-up'.
When Tim challenged her, she had been angry because she
felt incompetent. She then realized that being on the same
committee would be muddling while still in counselling,
and even when it finished it would be sensible to wait
some months. She also decided that there were other ways
of sharing her expertise with the executive committee.

It is probable that supervisor and supervisee and trainer and
trainee can work together, but this should not be presumed and
needs discussion.

Some counsellors look for counsellor/therapists and supervisors in another city. For instance, Leeds and Sheffield are far
enough apart for counsellors not necessarily to know peers in
the neighbouring city. However, there are practical consequences
with the time spent in travelling resulting in loss of earnings.
Another solution for counsellors in a neighbourhood where there
are few suitably experienced supervisors is to use someone who
was previously their counsellor/therapist. Some counsellors see
this as unacceptable, believing that the transference relationship

may still exist and would interfere with the supervisory process. Other counsellors do accept such a change in role, but insist on a break between the two relationships of at least a year. This is to try to ensure that the request for supervision is not an unconscious desire to continue the counselling. This would also be discussed in the first meeting to ascertain whether a supervisory relationship is advisable and would work. One consequence of this situation is that the counsellor loses his or her personal counsellor and cannot return to this relationship if the need arises. At that point she or he would have to seek alternative sources of support.

Counsellors vary about providing, if asked, the names of other practitioners in the neighbourhood. Potential clients might request this either because the counsellor they have approached has a waiting-list, or because they wish to 'shop around'. A reason for not giving names is that suggestions might be taken as recommendations or even advice which could result in recrimination, if not litigation, should the client be dissatisfied or worse, suffer abuse. A disclaimer would make it less likely that litigation would be successful. Another reason, though less defensible, is that some counsellors see all others as rivals for a limited source of clients. There is no doubt that envy does exist between practitioners. However, one of the advantages of seeking counselling in the private sector is that a client has a choice, even though this is limited in some areas of the country. For this reason alone a counsellor should at least direct a potential client to a directory such as that published by BAC, or advise that the BAC office will send out a list of practising counsellors in any region when requested to do so. In a recent survey of counsellors whose names are in the 1991/1992 BAC CPRD it was found that while 18 per cent did not receive any referrals as a result of their name being in the directory, those who did received an average of seven in the year (Palmer 1993). This survey found that most counsellors receive calls that were not followed up. This may be because potential clients do use the directory to 'shop around'.

REFERRALS FROM INDIVIDUALS, AGENCIES AND ORGANIZATIONS

It was mentioned in an earlier chapter that the majority of clients are self-referred. However, there are individuals, agencies and organizations who direct clients to counsellors. Some make referrals and others suggest that counselling might be helpful and supply some names. Examples of the former group are GPs, psychiatrists, hospital *in vitro* fertilization (IVF) programmes, Employee Assistance Programmes (EAPs), employers/bosses, religious organizations, and counsellor/therapists; examples of the latter are local colleagues (see above), local volunteer or work-based counselling services, RELATE, MIND, social workers and probation officers and, again, religious organizations.

Power is a significant issue in the referral process. Any potential client can perceive the referrer as both knowledgeable and powerful and this must be recognized. Clients may agree to come to a counsellor because they feel they must obey the person referring, or because they believe that she or he 'knows best' or is always right. These are not good reasons for choosing counselling. It is important, therefore, to try and ascertain why a client agreed to the suggestion or 'command' of someone else.

Each of the different sources of referral mentioned presents particular issues. In the case of a medical referral, the client is usually the employer of the counsellor. An exception to this is where couples are taking part in an IVF programme. The Human Fertilisation and Embryology Act 1990 requires that all people considering using these new reproductive techniques and those 'donating gametes' be 'given a suitable opportunity to receive proper counselling'. This can be undertaken by full-time employees of the hospital providing the treatment, but already counsellors in the private sector are being employed to do this work, particularly in the area of surrogacy, where it is recommended that the counsellor should be independent. In these instances the patient is paying the hospital and the counselling is being sub-contracted. The hospital is the employer and the counsellor's task is to assess and report on the genetic and host couples' 'psychological suitability' (King's Fund 1991) to take part in a surrogacy-treatment programme. They are therefore involved in the crucial decision regarding a couple's acceptance or refusal on to the treatment programme. This gives the counsellor real power and a dual role, which is normally absent in the counselling relationship, and which will affect the whole process. As yet this experience is limited, since the Act is relatively new and few counsellors from the independent sector have been employed. A great many details about good practice have still to be worked out. This is one of several situations where an Authority, often with little knowledge of counselling, chooses the counsellors and needs guidance on the ethics and good practice.

If the hospital is the employer, as in IVF counselling, a report is required. In any case, this is the expectation of medical practitioners, since it is normal medical procedure. They expect to give a written report with details about the client when referring, and similarly to receive a report from the counsellor. Both these practices are alien to many counsellors. They often prefer to meet a client without carrying preconceived ideas from someone else. Although this can be achieved by not reading the report until after the assessment session, it remains an issue. It exists and has to be read between the assessment and the contracting. The reluctance of some counsellors to write reports is related to the issues of confidentiality and abuse of power. Any unshared information gives the counsellor power and is contradictory to any egalitarian aims. One practice that ensures that the client is involved is to let clients see anything that is written and to jointly write the report, ensuring they have a copy. The latter is in line with current medical practice in any case, as a result of the Access to Health Records Act 1990.

Medical professionals can make good referrals, particularly if they have met counsellors and discovered the type of problems that are suitable for counselling, or if they have received some training about counselling and psychotherapy. More university medical courses now include interpersonal-skills training, and as a result counselling is beginning to be better understood, although there is a long way to go. However, counsellors have to beware. The referral may reflect the hopelessness of the doctors, so it only happens when all else has failed, rather than because counselling is the appropriate intervention for a particular problem.

It is not only medical practitioners who refer people when all else has failed. Employers also do so, sometimes with the added threat that unless the employee goes to a counsellor there will be no job. Understandably, clients resent this treatment. They may also resent a referral being made when they believe that their employer is 'passing the buck' and is avoiding offering them direct help, 'fobbing them off' instead with a counsellor. This also occurs when a member of the heirarchy of a religious organization, such as a bishop, makes referrals. In these situations counselling is unlikely to be effective, unless the resentments are recognized and worked with by the counsellor. This recognition and discussion can result in clients making a positive decision to enter counselling for themselves and not because someone is dictating that they should.

Needless to say, employers also make good referrals, but as there is usually no contract between the counsellor and the client's employer, and the employer may be paying, much needs to be clarified. It has to be made clear to employers that the counselling relationship is totally confidential and they will not receive a report. Any communication will be initiated by the client. Obviously the client also needs to know that this will be the case.

Counsellors in the independent sector frequently discuss the wisdom of accepting clients who do not pay their own fees. The 'benevolence' of the employer may need to be questioned. It may be a response to an unconscious communication by the client, and it will certainly have effects on the client. This is illustrated in the following vignette:

> Andrew had been referred to Sue, a counsellor, by his employer who, knowing that he was hard up, offered to pay his fees. Sue did not usually accept clients who were unable to pay their own fees. She told Andrew this, but discovered in the assessment session that Andrew's net income was extremely low. She felt sorry for him and his family and decided to accept payment from his employer. She did ask that Andrew should be given the money to pay her. This seemed preferable to either invoicing his employer direct or through Andrew.
>
> As time went by she realized that Andrew frequently told her of people who gave him unsolicited presents. There were also stories of his being the 'poorly' member of the family. He admitted that he had often feigned illness to stay off school and be with his mother on his own. Gradually Sue began to wonder if she and Andrew's employer were both caught up in a pattern of relating which started in his childhood. Did he only feel loved if people made him special by giving him things? Had he learnt early that it

was when his mother felt worried and sorry for him that he got attention?

With these insights Sue began to help Andrew unravel how he related to authority figures. Andrew gradually recognized that his boss was paying for his sessions because he felt sorry for him. He also realized that he was angry with everyone who related to him that way. Indeed, he was punishing his boss by letting him pay for his sessions.

Andrew was genuinely short of money, but he did not want to continue receiving gifts because he made people feel sorry for him. The dilemma for them both was how he should take over the responsibility of giving himself the 'gift' of counselling support. If Sue dropped her fees to the point where he could afford them, he was the recipient of benevolence again. The solution was to reduce his sessions from an hour to three quarters of an hour and for Andrew to pay for these sessions for himself.

There is no single response to an employer who offers to pay fees. Some counsellors do not accept such referrals; others do; others suggest the client pays part of the fee; and others have a lower fee for genuine hardship rather than involve another party. Some follow the practice described in the vignette, where this method of payment is accepted but its meanings explored with the client. There is a particular problem of parents of young adults paying fees: this was discussed in Chapter 4.

Occasionally clients referred by their employer are concerned to set up a meeting of the three people involved. This may well reflect the client's feeling of powerlessness and belief that the counsellor is powerful. Such a meeting is rarely useful. It is much more important to explore the reasons for the request. Is it fear of the employer? Or even a fear of the counsellor, the client perhaps believing that the employer will also be intimidated? In time this exploration should enable clients to exert their own power. It often helps clients to imagine and think through the meeting, looking at what outcome is sought. Employers also sometimes ask for a meeting about the client with the counsellor, with or without the client present. This must be firmly resisted.

As I have shown there are disadvantages to clients who reach a counsellor via their employer. In particular, they have not chosen the counsellor themselves and rely on the judgement of their employer. The employer may not have checked that the counsellor abides by a code of ethics and belongs to an organization with a complaints procedure. If the opportunity arises, counsellors should guide an employer in the questions to be asked.

A recent development, which was mentioned briefly in Chapter 2, is referrals through EAPs. These organizations draw up a contract between themselves and a company, offering the company's employees a confidential counselling service usually with a limited number of sessions (from three to eight sessions among the companies I know). The EAPs also draw up a contract with the counsellors, in which, generally, the counsellor undertakes to offer short-term counselling; to provide a written report; to adhere to a professional code of ethics and practice (such as BAC); and to have adequate public liability insurance and professional indemnity. In addition, there may be a clause prohibiting self-referral of the company employee in the event of their needing longer-term counselling. The range of problems for which counselling is offered can be very varied. For instance: marital and family problems, relationship difficulties, stress, substance abuse, redundancy, and in the case of employees in post offices, banks, betting shops and building societies, acute anxiety following a burglary or violent attack at work. People in the police force and fire and ambulance services similarly may suffer acute or even chronic anxiety after attending a major accident.

It makes economic sense for small companies or larger companies with many small branches up and down the country, to employ an EAP rather than set up their own counselling service. However, it can be seen from the range of problems that the work can be very difficult and short-term counselling may be grossly inadequate. Time and again I have found that employees who have witnessed a violent raid and subsequently suffered acute and prolonged anxiety, need considerable help with unresolved grief. It seems that the losses associated with a raid, such as loss of security, control, and expectations, evoke loss(es) from the past. Three to eight sessions is frequently inadequate for this type of work. If the counsellor's contract prohibits further sessions by the contracted counsellor, then another loss may be introduced far too early. In these situations it is irresponsible to make a short-term intervention. The decision to make no intervention rather than offer a short-term contract must be made at the assessment session and the client referred back to the EAP. Another difficulty for counsellors employed by EAPs is: who carries the clinical responsibility? Is it the counsellor or the organization? This needs to be clarified, particularly if the organization employs its own clinical advisers.

There are other problems associated with this type of work, some of which are similar to those for client's referred directly by their employer. Once again clients are not choosing their counsellor, and written reports are required. Some organizations ask the counsellor to approach the client rather than vice versa, which is normal practice. Most critically, it is often not clear to the company employee how and where to make complaints if the work is unsatisfactory or abusive. Indeed, the information leaflets given to the company employees often make no mention of codes of ethics and complaints procedures. Clearly some education needs to be undertaken in this area.

Occasionally counsellor/therapists themselves make referrals, particularly in situations where they are unable to continue working with clients, for instance, when a life-crisis makes work inadvisable or illness makes it impossible. In the extreme, a counsellor's death means clients have to be referred to someone else (see Chapter 3). In all these instances referral is necessary, partly because the work is incomplete, and partly because the sudden loss of the counsellor is likely to create its own grief and could also re-evoke unresolved past grief. It is most likely that a small number of counsellors will share the counselling commitments of the counsellor who has stopped working; therefore specific counsellors will be asked to take on particular clients. This removes the client's choice, which needs to be recognized. The client can subsequently be enabled to find someone of his or her own choice if so wished. In this situation it is extremely difficult to be certain whether the dissatisfaction with the new counsellor reflects the anger of the client at having to move or whether it is a genuine mismatch. It is essential to be aware of both possibilities and help clients find the best solution for themselves. With this type of referral the counsellor will be briefed on what has caused the sudden end of the previous counselling relationship. Practice varies on whether any more detail, for instance from the counselling notes, is acquired at this point. The majority of counsellors handle this as with medical referrals: they make up their own minds about the client rather than be influenced by someone else's opinion.

I have previously noted that some organizations and individuals do give people the names of counsellors. Although not strictly speaking referrals, these need to be handled in the same way. For instance, it is important to check why a particular suggestion of a counsellor was followed up. There may be issues of power to be explored. It is also essential for those concerned to discover what has been said about counselling and about counsellors in general, as well as specifically about themselves. The most appropriate referrals tend to come from people who have had training in counselling or counselling skills. Examples are social workers, probation officers, priests, and professional and voluntary counsellors. A recent development has been that those employed in counselling services in Institutions of Higher and Further Education suggest to staff, who consult them, that they seek further help in the independent sector. It is a measure of the stress in these institutions, and of the greater acceptance of counselling, that their services have been inundated with work. In some instances this has resulted in limits on the number of sessions available to clients, and particularly for staff. Although short-term counselling may be offered, the member of staff is then encouraged to move into the independent sector if further work is needed. In this instance, clients arrive with some knowledge of counselling, and feelings about the transition. They are likely to compare the counsellors. These issues will be the basis of the early work and may make it more difficult to form a therapeutic alliance.

RELATIONSHIP WITH OTHER PROFESSIONALS

Unless they positively plan to do so, counsellors in independent practice rarely meet other professionals except as clients. On occasion they are asked to speak to a group of professionals, but it is more likely that they will be the ones arranging the meetings. Such activities are in themselves worth while, particularly when starting an independent practice (Kopp 1977: 24), and can also lead to a greater number of appropriate referrals.

Some counsellors choose to have limited contact with other professionals. For some, the reason for this is a deliberate decision to maintain anonymity, because fellow professionals are a very likely source of clients. Another reason for some is that they have moved into the independent sector to avoid the seemingly endless negotiations, arguments and frustrations of working in agencies and institutions. Yet other counsellors are very skilled in working with clients but are aware they have few skills for engaging in the politics of the external world. These people wisely protect themselves without feeling deficient for avoiding other professionals.

On rare occasions a client may suggest that their solicitor contact their counsellor, when a report is required in legal proceedings. For example, if a client is charged with and pleading guilty to sexual offences, the defence barrister may be concerned to demonstrate that his or her client has undertaken counselling voluntarily and is thereby taking responsibility. Counsellors have to decide for themselves what is ethical and appropriate in discussion with the clients and their solicitors, in a situation that challenges the core ethic of confidentiality. The very existence of legal proceedings affects the nature of the counselling relationship, even before a counsellor has become involved in writing reports. In general, lawyers know little about counselling and these interactions can be a valuable method of imparting information.

There is no doubt that professionals in other fields do bring work to counsellors. However, this is not the only, nor the main reason why counsellors need to meet other professionals. This is that these contacts provide other avenues of interest and self-expression (see Chapter 3) that counteract the potential isolation. A popular way of achieving this is to combine training with counselling, either as a trainer or as a trainee on a course. Working as a trainer will be looked at in detail in the next section of this chapter.

There are many courses available to counsellors. All will widen counsellors' networks of support, bringing them into contact with peers, professionals who use counselling skills in their work, and others who are interested. The choice of courses is important, because counsellors need both to maintain their continuing professional development and to give themselves enjoyment and refreshment. These two aims are not mutually exclusive, but a particular course may fulfil one more than the other. It is important overall that in any year both these needs must be met adequately.

RELATIONSHIPS WITHIN THE TRAINING FIELD

Many people in other walks of life who are self-employed are also involved in training or teaching. For instance, many crafts-people such as potters, artists and writers also work as tutors in their field. The different activity is refreshing; it is reward-ing to introduce new knowledge and skills to highly motivated people; it counteracts the isolation of being self-employed; and it broadens the money-earning base. The same applies to counsellors, with the additional attraction of possibly earning more per hour for training. This enables them to offer some concessionary places to the low paid or unemployed. Counsel-lors should not work as trainers unless they have the necessary skills and knowledge. BAC has recently introduced a scheme to accredit trainers and has a Code of Ethics and Practice for Trainers with sections relating to counselling and counselling skills.

The range of courses run by counsellors is huge, reflecting both their varied backgrounds and the diversity of models of psychological functioning used. Counsellors may be employed by organizations to teach topics such as counselling, counselling skills, loss and bereavement counselling, managing conflict and stress, and many more topics to groups of professionals. These groups may be limited to a specific profession or may incorporate many. For example, hospitals may provide a course for nursing staff alone, or they may make this available to all medical person-nel, resulting in a mixed group of nurses, speech therapists, physiotherapists, radiographers and social workers. Other organ-izations that arrange such courses for their personnel are schools, church organizations, the Family Health Services Authority, the probation service and social services. The content may be directed towards introducing or improving skills, or can emphasize well-being and self-knowledge; for example, stress management, lifeskills, and family patterning. These may be provided for employees as part of their overall welfare provision.

These type of courses are also found in colleges of Further and Higher Education, as are those on particular theoretical ap-proaches including gestalt, transactional analysis, psychosynthesis and neuro-linguistic programming. Colleges have recognized the seemingly insatiable demand for counselling courses and use them as a good source of income. They arrange the courses and then sub-contract the training, often to counsellors in the independent sector. When costing this type of work it is important for a counsellor to remember to allow for the preparation and debriefing time as well as actual contact hours, and to recognize that the overheads for running the practice continue whether in the counselling premises or elsewhere. Problems can arise when the counsellor/trainer is employed by someone who is not a counsellor. Administrators and professionals from other areas bring their own standards and requirements to the work, which may be in conflict with those of counsellors. Before undertaking this work it is important for counsellors to check the objectives of the commissioning organization and ensure they are not in conflict with their own, nor with those of their code of ethics and practice as a trainer. The following is a typical example of the dilemmas that can arise when considering running a course for an organization:

Betty was approached by an acquaintance, Ted, who taught in a FE college, asking if she would be a tutor on a course he was arranging. It was to be held one evening a week for two terms and was entitled 'An Introduction to Counselling Skills'. The course was to be open to anyone, because this was the policy of the college, and there was a syllabus to be covered. This syllabus had already been agreed the previous year and was identical to the daytime course the college was also running. There would be a certificate at the end. Betty was interested and suggested she should meet members of the college staff.

The meeting was attended by two members of the college, Ted and an administrator. In the ensuing discussion Betty thought that the syllabus had been well-designed, and was pleased to hear that the costing included the costs of the supervision of a trainer. But she was very concerned when she learnt that the plan was for a single tutor, who was to work alone with a minimum of 18 people.

She expressed concern that there was no co-tutor, whom she regarded as essential, particularly because of the open access. She was told that the course was not viable unless there were 18 members; it would be too expensive if they costed it on the basis of two tutors; and that the trainer on the day course was happy to work alone. Betty was also concerned about the certificate that would be awarded.

Was it simply a recognition of the completion of the course? Or was it awarded if a certain standard had been achieved? If it was the latter, what were the criteria and who acted as moderator? The responses to these questions were not satisfactory so she withdrew.

In this example the counsellor had different expectations from the lecturer. Teachers expect to work with large groups on their own, whereas Betty would not undertake any training work without a co-trainer, no matter how small the group, because this was unethical in view of the strong feelings that can be evoked on an experiential course. The introduction to the BAC Code of Ethics for Trainers recommends working with a co-trainer and that the group size should be limited and linked to the number of trainers. She was also in conflict with the administrator whose sole concern was with economic viability. Finally another counsellor, a competitor, was prepared to work in ways which Betty considered to be unprofessional. Sometimes a self-employed counsellor can feel very isolated when economic needs conflict with professional standards. Here a peer-group can be a useful support in maintaining standards.

It is similarly important to check the objectives, codes of practice, syllabus, modes of teaching, and methods of appraisal when being employed as a supervisor of trainers – another area of work open to counsellors in independent practice. It is important to give sufficient forethought before accepting this kind of work so as not to find oneself associated with a course that is unprofessional in its practice, whatever the economic attractions. Many more college tutors are prepared to learn the professional ways of running counselling courses.

Another possibility is for counsellors to arrange their own courses as a private enterprise, finding their own venue, doing their own publicity, costing and administration, and selecting topics for which there is a market. However, most of those involved in this way tend to be trainers who do some counselling work rather than vice versa.

The merit of involvement in courses is that knowledge of counselling and counsellors is extended to a wider group both of professionals and the general public. This in turn results in a more informed public who are, after all, the source of work. Members of courses sometimes become clients themselves, although this needs careful thought (see Chapter 2); and they generate a wider interest in counselling, including recommending it to friends, family and colleagues. Sometimes they are in a position professionally to make referrals or suggest counselling to their clients or patients. As can be seen, running courses results in increased contacts and thereby generates work.

Running courses also generate revenue. It will be clear from the discussion of fees in Chapter 4 that it is difficult for counsellors in full-time private practice to create enough income by only working with clients, if they are conscientious about not taking on too many and are also concerned to look after themselves. A combination of one-to-one work and a small amount of training work both increases earnings and fulfils the need to have other interests. It is also a way of counteracting the isolation.

A number of the organizations which employ counsellors as trainers also use them as consultants; in particular to help in team-building and to act as facilitators and conciliators in resolving a conflict. From the counsellor's viewpoint this is another way of broadcasting the particular skills of counselling and again results in publicity, if not work.

RELATIONSHIP WITH TRAINING ORGANIZATIONS WITHIN THE PROFESSION

One reason for the imbalance between counsellor provision in London and the neighbouring counties and the rest of the UK is the number of training bodies in London. This is true for counselling, psychotherapy and psychoanalysis; the London area has many more training courses, training therapists and a far greater network of counsellors. It is possible to undertake initial training in the provinces, but almost all advanced training takes place in London. Obviously, the commitment of time is far less for someone travelling within London or from the home counties to London than from further afield. This has implications for private practitioners funding their own continuing professional development (CPD).

This concentration of training bodies and counsellors in London might appear to give them immense power. However, some of the training societies are also very insular, with therapists of a like mind rarely being challenged by other viewpoints. At times this results in an élitism in which their approaches and rules are seen as good practice and all others falling short. This can be compounded by idealization by practitioners in the provinces, some of whom have travelled to London for training, believing that they were being offered a superior service. This at least needs questioning.

A number of trainers coming from London to the provinces have been amazed at, if not disapproving of, the confused boundaries that have necessarily arisen when the network of counsellors is very small. These attitudes can inhibit a dialogue and an openness to considering whether there is something to be learnt from the practices that have evolved outside London. The 'London' rules about boundaries, for instance, may be far too rigid; excellent, but different practice, has evolved outside London, with no evidence that the work has been compromised by modified rules. It would be unfortunate if the rifts that occurred in the early history of psychoanalysis were to be repeated in counselling because of rigidity and arrogance.

Some London-based organizations have recognized the opportunity for training in the provinces and started giving lectures and running courses. An example of this is the Institute of Psycho-Analysis which has arranged a series of public lectures in Leeds and an Introductory Course on Psychoanalytic Approaches, using members of the British Psycho-Analytical Society as lecturers. While they have done this because of a perceived need and the lectures are well-attended, this can be seen as somewhat patronizing if the exchanges are only one-way. There are training bodies running excellent courses who have their centres in the provinces, for instance the Institute of Group Analysis in Manchester, the Group Relations Training Association and the Scottish Institute of Human Relations in Edinburgh, and the Association for Person-Centred Therapy Scotland in Glasgow. They all have experience to share of different but equally professional practice, from which everyone can learn. Perhaps some of the provincial training bodies need to invite the longer established London-based organizations to attend seminars which they organize, with the aim of encouraging discussion on the modified ways of working.

Other organizations have recognized the problem and although bringing their own courses, have used local counsellors as trainers and supervisors. Westminster Pastoral Foundation is one such

London-based organization that has done this recently, setting up a base in Leeds (WPF Counselling North). This initiative, while welcomed locally, does maintain the illusion that the London-based courses are the best by importing the course evolved by London practitioners rather than designing a new course based on the practice that has evolved in Leeds. They can also undermine local initiatives by competing with the local counselling and psychotherapy associations for the same small group of counsellors and psychotherapists. What is needed is recognition of the importance of cross-fertilization and a system of training which gives equivalency to a wide range of courses both in London and the provinces.

DIFFICULTIES

A number of difficulties in relationships with other workers has already been highlighted in this and previous chapters. No job is without its stresses. For some counsellors in the independent sector there may be isolation, which has been mentioned; but there are also issues relating to competition and marginalization.

In the business world the market is finite, though fluctuating in parallel with the economy. In the private counselling sector at present, demand exceeds supply, but this will not always be the case. It is important that counsellors recognize that when they set up in independent practice they become another competitor for this finite market. It is very stressful to be concerned over whether enough revenue is being generated to cover overheads. Care has to be taken that the stress of competition does not result in bad practice; for instance, accepting the role of tutor on a training course which compromises standards, or accepting too many clients and not taking care of oneself.

For some the competition results in envy. This can also result in bad practice, which cannot be challenged or controlled at present. In a 'cut-throat' world some would think it foolish to suggest to clients that they should 'shop around' before selecting a counsellor. Confidentiality means that counsellors are not likely to know what libellous statements are made about them by another counsellor behind closed doors. Of course, this is unscrupulous and unethical, but without a common Code of Ethics and Practice and complaints procedure, and standards of good practice for all counsellors in independent practice, bad practice can go unchallenged. The very challenge needs a formal and agreed procedure if it in turn is not to promote further stress and organizational difficulty.

Envy also exists between the different sectors. The grass is always greener elsewhere! Institutionally based counsellors sometimes envy those in independent practice and vice versa. Is it envy that brings the charge from Pilgrim (1992) that private practice is unethical and exploitative? He suggests that it is unethical to exclude people 'who are already physically or emotionally distressed' from help because they cannot afford a fee, or to 'impoverish' them further by accepting payment. The powerful counter-argument to this is discussed by Rowan (1992) and centres round the cost of institutional counselling being hidden and kept distant from the client, but none the less there. He also suggests that there is ambiguity in the public sector over for whom the counsellor is actually working. In the private sector this is unambiguous; the counsellor works solely for the client.

Counsellors in the independent sector can feel marginalized and undervalued despite efforts to interest and involve other professionals. Few referrals come from professionals in other fields, even though efforts are made to interact with those in obvious need of counselling and those with the resources to employ a counsellor. Medical practitioners in particular make few referrals, despite the fact that they may refer their patients privately for medical interventions. The reasons are probably lack of knowledge and prejudice on the doctor's part, and perhaps quite justifiable caution. On occasions it is impossible to work with a client because of the hostility of his or her GP or psychiatrist.

Counsellors have a major role in overcoming this hostility by educating other professionals, so that they understand what counselling is and that counsellors are not actually in competition with them, but want to co-operate in the best interests of the client. An even more important task for all professional counsellors is to ensure that counselling becomes a profession with an accepted and clear system of training and qualifications, codes of ethics and practice, complaints procedures and monitoring of good practice. Only then can other professionals feel safe in making referrals. I will discuss this in detail in the final chapter.

· SIX ·

A critique of counselling in independent practice

There is a central dilemma for all counsellors working in independent practice. No matter how professional, competent and well-trained individual counsellors are in their work, counselling is not currently considered a profession. To some extent, this is also problematic for those working in other contexts, but it is at its most acute in independent practice. There is no employer to hire counsellors of an appropriate standard and to fire those who behave unprofessionally. At the moment, anyone can call him or herself a 'counsellor', and earn money that way. Clients can therefore unknowingly place themselves in a situation where their counsellor has little if any training and qualifications, and they have few consumer rights and little redress if they are abused, financially, emotionally or sexually. This is clearly an unsatisfactory situation for responsible practitioners and clients alike. It is little wonder that other professionals are reluctant to refer when there is such a plethora of theories and methods of counselling and no control over the use of the title 'counsellor'.

The safety of the general public in the future depends at least on the formation of a Register if not actual Chartering. Such a step will include control of standards and monitoring of the work. It is expected that a voluntary Register will come into being during 1994.

QUALIFICATIONS AND REGISTRATION

The current counselling world is complex. The 1993 BAC *Counselling and Psychotherapy Resources Directory* (CPRD) lists some 116

organizations to which counsellors named in the directory belong and from whom they may have received training. The
majority of training courses will not be included, because many
are organized by local colleges. Few of these are recognized by
BAC or by any other validating body. The current CPRD also
lists 76 organizations who are members of the United Kingdom
Conference for Psychotherapy (UKCP), some of which overlap
with those described above, all with their own codes of ethics
and practice. The complexity is further demonstrated in a recent
survey of its members by BAC. Twenty-four different models of
'psychological functioning' were named and members were asked
to indicate which one best described their preferred model.
Twenty-three of these are named as theoretical approaches by
counsellors with their name in the BAC 1993 CPRD; the approach not mentioned is Sullivanian. However, this does not
give a complete picture; there are 120 other approaches mentioned by counsellors in this directory. A total of 143 are listed
in Table 6.1; those marked with an asterisk are the models of
psychological functioning named in the BAC survey. This table
illustrates that there is an extensive range of approaches, with
only a small proportion obviously linking with the descriptions of
the three main schools of counselling mentioned in Chapter 1.

Closer examination reveals that some of these theoretical
models are essentially the same described by different names;
for instance Attachment and Bowlby, or Ericksonian and
Ericksonian hypnotherapy, or person-centred and client-centred;
but only those with sufficient knowledge could know this. At
least one approach, described as theoretical by the counsellor,
is simply the name of an author of a book, Louise Hay, who has
written *You Can Heal Your Life* (Hay 1988). There is no indication
from details of qualifications and training that the counsellor
concerned has attended any training course linked with the book.
This is only one example of the stated theoretical approach not
appearing to link with any training course or qualification, and
therefore lacking any real substance or meaning. To complicate
matters further, some counsellors have listed as many as six
theoretical approaches, and the validity of such statements is
clearly open to question and challenge. The compilers of the
CPRD understandably make no attempt to describe all these
different theories. It is doubtful whether any counsellor could
do so. How then can potential clients find out about them in

Table 6.1 Theoretical Approaches to Counselling found in *Counselling and Psychotherapy Resources Directory 1993* (CPRD)

Adlerian*
Affirmative
Analytic
Analytic middle group
Applied family therapy
Applied psychoanalysis
Artwork
Astrological
Attachment
Balint
Behaviour/learning theory*
Behaviour modification
Behavioural sex therapy
Biodynamic
Bioenergetics
Body centred
Body oriented
Bodywork
Bowlby
Breathwork
Brief psychotherapy
Broad
Christian counselling
Client-centred counselling
Clinical and pastoral counselling
Co-counselling*
Co-dependency
Cognitive*
Cognitive analytic therapy (CAT)
Cognitive-behavioural*
Cognitive hypnotherapy
Cognitive psychotherapeutic
    approach
Cognitive strategy
Contemporary post-Jungian
    developmental theory
Contribution training
Core process
Counselling psychology
Development skills
Developmental

Eclectic*
Eclectic analytical (British
    school)
Egan
Elman
English school
Ericksonian
Ericksonian hypnotherapy
Existential*
Experiential-constructivist
Expressive
Family system
Family therapy
Feminist
Feminist systemic integrative
Feuerstein instrumental
    enrichment
Freudian (psychodynamic)*
Generic
Gestalt*
Grofian
Group analytic therapy
Group psychodynamic
David Grove
Guided affective imagery
Louise Hay
Healing the inner child
Holistic
Karen Horney
Humanistic
Human social functioning
Hypnoanalysis
Hypnotherapy
Imagery
Imaginal
Independent Freudian
Inner healing
Integral therapy
Integrated
Integrated psychodynamic-
    behavioural

Table 6.1 (Cont.)

Integrative
Interactional
Jungian (psychodynamic)*
Kleinian (psychodynamic)*
Lacanian psychoanalysis
Medical hypnosis
Meditation
Metaphor therapy
Metapsychology
Alice Miller focus
Mind/body connection
Mind clearing
Minnesota model
Mixed
Multimedia art therapy
Multimodal therapy*
Nelson Jones
Neo-Freudian (Erich Fromm)
Neo-Reichian
Neuro-linguistic programming
    (NLP)
Object relations
    (psychodynamic)*
Pellin
Performative
Person-centred*
Personal construct psychology
    (PCP)
Phenomenonological
Play therapy
Pluralistic
Positive imaging
Post-Freudian
Primal integration*
Primal therapy*

Problem management
Problem solving
Process oriented
Process oriented psychology
Psychoanalytic
Psychoanalytic, middle group
Psycho-developmental
Psychodrama
Psychodynamic*
Psycho-spiritual
Psychosynthesis*
Rational-emotive therapy (RET)*
Reality therapy
Redecision therapy
Regression and integrational
Reichian
Relaxation
Remedial
Rogerian
Sand play
Shamanistic
Social learning theory
Sociometry
Spiritual
Systemic process-oriented
    psychology
Systems theory*
Traditional
Transactional analysis (TA)*
Transpersonal*
Voice dialogue
Wide influences
Will and Wrate
Winnicottian
Woman

Note: *Theoretical approaches included in BAC Membership Survey 1993.

order to make an informed choice? Clients who try to seek
understandable information are met instead with a confusing
array of seemingly meaningless labels. To some extent, clients
can only decide if a counsellor suits them by working with them,
but this is no justification for the existing situation that denies
consumers accurate information. If a counsellor does not suit,
the client can leave but this will have involved loss of money,
time and sometimes hope. The onus should be on counsellors
to describe accurately and in detail how they work. The most
suitable medium for this is in a pre-counselling leaflet (see
Chapter 3). BAC should also consider whether the directory
offers sufficient guidance regarding theoretical approaches.
Greater selectivity is also needed about what constitutes an acceptable approach. If these measures are to have real meaning
and substance, one criterion for inclusion must be to have had
a substantial training. A weekend course, or reading a book or
manual, is not sufficient, but the question of what is substantial
remains.

Another question for potential clients is whether there is one
organization that can direct them to all the counsellors in the
country. The answer is no. While the BAC directory has the
most comprehensive list, the Association of Humanistic Psychotherapy Practitioners and the Institute of Psychosexual Medicine
both supply names of counsellors and therapists, as do a number
of other training organizations and accrediting bodies. Having
found names of counsellors, the client will then need to know
if a particular standard of practice can be expected. The situation at the moment is that the media is raising the issue of lack
of standards through articles and TV and radio programmes, and
offering guidance on what should be expected (see Chapter 4).
The Introduction to the 1993 CPRD also lists appropriate questions. In any occupation which has either an assessment process, a registration scheme, or a Charter, such questions would
be unnecessary. We do not expect to have to check on the
qualifications of bus drivers or medical practitioners! We assume
that their employer or professional association will ensure that
the expert has sufficient qualifications, a suitable length of training
and/or apprenticeship, and, in the case of the professions, has
met certain professional requirements, such as having professional indemnity insurance, and having their work supervised.
This should also be true for counselling, psychotherapy and

psychoanalysis, although as I have shown the reality is very different.

There have been some attempts to clarify and resolve the confusion. The UK Government set up a commission after there had been considerable public outcry about scientology. Its report (Foster 1971) recommended legislation to control psychotherapy in the UK. In 1978 the Sieghart Report (Report of a Profession's Working Party) recommended indicative registration and a council for psychotherapists. In 1981 a Private Member's Bill was introduced to the House of Commons by Graham Bright, MP, to regulate the practice and profession of psychotherapy and related disciplines, but this was talked out at its second reading. At this time the Department of Health and Social Security stated the Government would not act until the profession could agree on both the need for a professional register and its membership (Dyne 1988). BAC organized a symposium in 1982 to further discuss the Foster and Sieghart reports. The outcome was to postpone registration in favour of forming a Standing Conference as a forum for all the psychotherapies. For the next seven years, annual conferences, known as the Rugby Psychotherapy Conferences, then took place, with the formation of the United Kingdom Standing Conference for Psychotherapy (UKSCP) in 1989. In 1991 this body voted to form a Register of Psychotherapists, which finally came into being in 1993. From 1993 there has been a Registration Board which has created and now maintains a Register of Psychotherapists and checks that training is being properly validated. The standing conference has now been renamed the United Kingdom Conference for Psychotherapy (UKCP).

The brevity of this factual account masks the innumerable arguments and divisions that have occurred. As a result of disagreements over standards of training, a number of organizations representing psychoanalysts withdrew from the conference. Other organizations withdrew because they had a very small membership and so could not afford the subscription to the UKSCP, as it was named then. The remaining organizations have split into eight sections, reflecting considerable differences in training and interests. These groups are: analytical psychotherapy (the biggest group); behavioural psychotherapy; family, marital, sexual therapy; humanistic and integrative psychotherapy; hypnotherapy; analytical psychology; psycho-analytically based therapy with children; and experiential constructivist therapies. Each section has set its minimum standards for organizational membership and had these scrutinized by the other sections. Each organizational member then has to give evidence that their members reach these standards, and the list of their practising members will form the Preliminary List which in turn will become the basis of the Register. While disagreement is considerable in some areas, for instance whether all trainees must have their own therapy and if so how many times a week, there has been unanimity over psychotherapy being a post-graduate level profession.

One reason for this decision has been EEC pressure. One directive protects the rights of all professions with a graduate entry to practise in any EEC country without having to retrain. In the initial stage graduate entry necessitates a 'grandparent' clause so that long-established practitioners without the appropriate academic qualifications will be allowed to register. There is no agreement as yet on how long this transitional period will last before all trainees have to be graduates and have followed an approved training to be eligible for the Register. Undoubtedly this is a first step towards professionalization, but a second EEC directive requires each member country to establish a competent authority to set standards and control the awarding of professional qualifications. The UKCP does now have a standard for entry into the profession, but no profession exists without the means of disciplining members for malpractice, and without the ultimate sanction of being able to suspend someone from practice for varying lengths of time, up to and including the rest of their lives. The UKCP insists that all its organizational members have a Code of Ethics and procedures to deal with complaints and grievances. The UKCP has an 'umbrella' role ensuring that all the codes of the member organizations have common minimum standards. If a complaint is upheld, the individual is forbidden from stating that he or she is a member of the organization or a registered psychotherapist, but this does not stop him or her from working and even calling him or herself a psychotherapist. This will only end when there is a single National Register to which people must belong if they work as psychotherapists. This is equally true for counsellors.

It will be remembered that BAC organized the first symposium in Rugby. It has remained involved in the consultation process, but has not joined any of the sections of UKCP, remaining 'friends of the conference'. Recently BAC has taken the initiative to explore the 'desirability and feasibility of setting up a National (UK) Register for Counselling as the basis of a single, national, Government-recognized system of professional self-regulation for counselling which might lead eventually to Charter status' (National Register Working Party (UK) Consultative Document). Consultation has been between BAC, Westminster Pastoral Foundation, RELATE and the Confederation of Scottish Counselling Agencies (COSCA). These four organizations were chosen because they were all national bodies and had their own internal systems of accreditation and regulation. If these organizations were to merge their individual systems of self-regulation, this would be the first step towards a National Register. This is planned initially as a voluntary Register, which it is hoped will become a statutory Register. The drive for the National Register partly relates to concern about standards and partly, as with UKCP, as a response to the pressure from EEC directives. A credible system of self-regulation must have a register of members; a minimum standard for entry; a code of ethics and standards; a requirement for members to give evidence of continuing professional development; a complaints procedure and a body with the authority to investigate any breaches of the code of ethics and standards and to invoke sanctions. Whenever new sanctions or higher standards are introduced, there will be considerable unrest. This was the case when BAC introduced a much more rigorous accreditation scheme for counsellors in 1987. However, the Register must be seen to be effective to gain public credibility.

The most difficult issue to resolve is likely to be a minimum standard for entry. In setting this the following interrelated issues need to be considered:

Whether registered counsellors must be graduates;
The balance of theory to practice;
Whether counsellors have to be trained on specified accredited or recognized training courses;
Integration of National Vocational Qualification (NVQ) awards in Advice, Guidance and Counselling into the range of qualifications that can be credited;
Existing accreditation schemes;
Experience of licensing in the United States;

Rationalization of the range of theoretical approaches;
What is a minimum standard?

Whatever criteria are finally accepted there will have to be a
transition period and a 'grandparent' clause, exactly as there has
been for the psychotherapy register and for all other employment groups who have become chartered (e.g. engineers, psychologists, accountants, physiotherapists, architects, quantity
surveyors). The osteopaths are the employment group who have
most recently gained statutory regulation.

All National Registers and Chartered Societies set pre-entry
requirements. A major question is whether or not registered
counsellors must be graduates. There are a number of precedents
for this. First UKCP has decided that all registered psychotherapists
will be graduates. Second, a recent initiative by the British
Psychological Society (BPS), a chartered society, is to introduce
a Diploma in Counselling Psychology. A pre-entry requirement
for this course is to be a graduate. Completion of this diploma
will enable people to become counselling psychologists and to be
registered as a chartered psychologist. In the initial phase, counselling psychologists who can show the Board of Examiners
that their qualifications and experience are equivalent to the
Diploma will be awarded a Statement of Equivalence to the
Diploma, and hence also be able to become a chartered psychologist. Third, the system of licensing of counselling in most
of the USA is for graduates. The criteria for being licensed as a
counsellor varies from state to state, and not all have yet introduced this system of 'licensure'. However, the majority of those
that have insist that to be licensed, counsellors have to pass a
written examination (commonly either the National Board for
Certified Counselors [NCBB] exam or the National Academy of
Certified Clinical Medical Health Counselors [NACCMHC] exam),
have had two or more years of supervised work practice and
have a master's degree plus 60 hours of graduate study (Lee and
Six 1992). This system has created enormous problems in the
USA for voluntary organizations using volunteer counsellors, as
well as for other counsellors who have no formal academic
qualifications and have become good counsellors through a form
of apprenticeship. This will have involved receiving counselling
over an extended period of time; participating in courses on
theory and skills, and in others directed towards increased

self-knowledge. Many of those involved are extremely competent and yet not eligible for a licence, so they may not work as counsellors (Lee, personal communication). It will be important in the UK to devise a system without this rigidity or many well-respected counsellors would be debarred. For this reason, I believe that making possession of a degree a pre-entry requirement would be a mistake. Any system adopted should recognize an apprentice training and a considerable amount of supervised practice as being equivalent to academic qualifications. There is precedence for this in some universities where both practitioner and the conventional research doctorates are now being awarded.

If being a graduate is not a mandatory pre-entry requirement, a decision has to be made on another basis that sets a minimum standard of education in counselling theory and supervised practice and also provides a number of ways that this can be achieved using equivalency, accrediting prior learning, and a system of credit accumulation. A model for this exists in the recent initiative by the Department of Employment to establish National Vocational Qualification (NVQ) awards in Advice, Guidance and Counselling. Previous experiential learning in the work-place is acknowledged, assessed and accredited using Accreditation of Prior Learning (APL), which is then used as part of a credit accumulation system.

The aim of any Register should be to educate and raise standards so that the profession is enhanced. It should not primarily be an exclusionary process (Lee and Six 1992). The standard for entry should not be so low that organizations and individuals are accepted which compromise the standard and depreciate the Register. On the other hand, the standard should not be so high that few can become eligible. The standard has to be above the lowest common denominator if the profession is to be enhanced. Taking BAC as an example, because it has the largest membership, the lowest standard would be for all individual members who work as counsellors to be on the Register. The only requirement would be to adhere to the Codes of Ethics and Practice and therefore to be liable for disciplinary action if these codes were broken. However, it could be argued that this standard is too low because the only stipulation about training in the Code of Ethics and Practice for Counsellors is to have 'received adequate basic training' (Clause 2.3.2). This does not specify sufficiently the need for both theory and supervised practice. An alternative standard would be that set for accreditation (see Chapter 4). This application process is demanding and time-consuming. At present only 568 people out of a membership of approximately 10,000 are accredited, and only 301 of those with names in the 1993 CPRD are accredited counsellors. Additionally, there are another 25 accredited supervisors in this directory who will also be of a standard to be accredited as counsellors.

Another accreditation scheme for counsellors exists within BAC. This is for student counsellors and is administered by the Association for Student Counselling (ASC) (see Bell, forthcoming). Their requirements for accreditation are:

> To be employed as a 'designated student counsellor' for not less than eight hours per week;
> Either have completed an 'extensive counselling training course and the equivalent of one year's full-time work as a student counsellor'; or to have completed 'three years' work, full-time or equivalent, as a student counsellor' and give evidence of 'involvement in activities designed to promote professional and personal development';
> To receive 'regular and continuing consultative support, usually designated "supervision", for at least six months prior to application';
> To have attended 'conferences, courses, training events and workshops as part of on-going professional education. This may include personal therapy/counselling'.
>
> (ASC Guidelines and Requirements for
> Members Seeking Accreditation)

This scheme could be usefully adapted to all counsellors and would ensure a sensible and meaningful standard for the National Register. It allows for dual entry, one via a route that involves formal training and supervised practice, the alternative being via an apprenticeship route. Decisions on the definition of 'extensive counselling training' would still be needed, whether this be formal training on a course or the less formal training of the apprentice route.

This 'extensive counselling training' should include a minimum number of hours spent in studying counselling theory; in practising counselling skills; in supervised practice with clients; and in developing self-awareness. This could be accumulated by attending various courses and by carrying out practical work in counselling agencies, and could also use APL. This would be the apprentice route. Completion of a substantial course, meeting the requirements of the National Register, would be the alternative route. In time, the National Register would accredit or recognize courses which meet the training requirements for registered counsellors.

A discussion of training also raises the issue of the enormous variety of theoretical approaches. Is any theoretical approach to counselling acceptable for the National Register? Or should some be excluded? And how and who decides? There is no doubt that if those representing different theoretical approaches individually drew up their own code of ethics and practice, they would be incompatible. For instance, some approaches involve touch (e.g. Reichian) whereas some psychodynamic counsellors would have a total embargo on this. This difficulty has been resolved in UKCP by having different sections and could be used by those setting up a National Register, allowing each section to set its own standards within an agreed framework.

A more detailed analysis of all the theoretical approaches found in the 1993 BAC CPRD is shown in Table 6.2. All the approaches in this table were mentioned ten or more times. The most frequently mentioned theoretical approaches are psychodynamic (16.1 per cent), eclectic (12 per cent), Rogerian (9.8 per cent), and client/person centred (7.8 per cent). If the different approaches were reclassified into sections then the four obvious sections would be psychodynamic and psychoanalytic (including analytic, Freudian, Jungian, object relations, Kleinian and integrated); humanistic-existential (including Rogerian, client/person centred, humanistic, gestalt, integrative, transactional analysis, existential and psychosynthesis); cognitive-behavioural (including cognitive behavioural and rational-emotive therapy); and eclectic.

No matter how a National Register is sectionalized, the system of entry requirements should incorporate the NVQ awards. These have been established by the National Council for Vocational Qualifications (NCVQ) and set standards of competency for every industry. There are five levels in the framework with Level 1 being the simplest. Counselling comes within the general area of Advice, Guidance and Counselling and it is expected that qualifications will range through levels 2–5. These must be recognized and integrated into any accreditation scheme as one of

Table 6.2   Frequency that entrants in BAC CPRD 1993 refer to different theoretical approaches

Approach	Number	Percentage
Psychodynamic	504	16.1
Eclectic	377	12.0
Rogerian	305	9.7
Client/person centred	245	7.8
Gestalt	214	6.8
Humanistic	173	5.5
Analytic	167	5.3
Integrative	120	4.1
Transactional Analysis	114	3.6
Jungian	101	3.2
Psychoanalytic	70	2.2
Behavioural	55	1.7
Transpersonal	54	1.7
Existential	49	1.6
Psychosynthesis	49	1.6
Cognitive-behavioural	27	0.9
Egan	25	0.8
Object relations	25	0.8
Holistic	24	0.8
Freudian	20	0.6
Neuro-Linguistic Programming	20	0.6
Systemic	20	0.6
Hypnotherapy	19	0.6
Kleinian	17	0.5
Integrated	14	0.4

a range of qualifications which can be credited and accumulated to reach the pre-entry standard. A Level 4 NVQ qualification is unlikely to be sufficient on its own as a pre-entry requirement, because it is competency based and does not examine the whole context in which counselling as a profession is practised. The Department of Employment has now commissioned the NCVQ to conduct a feasibility study to discover whether a professional level can be introduced for Applied Psychology. This would be a Level 5 NVQ and counselling psychology would be one of the professions within this group. It is not clear whether this will go ahead and whether, as it is again competency based, it will be of a sufficient standard to be one of a range of acceptable pre-entry qualifications. However, Level 5 is to be equivalent to a Masters Degree in other disciplines, so it should be.

If a system of accreditation similar to ASC's is used for entry to the National Register, it would not represent a sufficiently high standard for counsellors in independent practice. As I stated in Chapter 4, all independent practitioners should be at least of a standard to be eligible for accreditation by BAC. However, this scheme has two merits. First, it is already in place, and second, it allows for both a formal and an informal training. If this scheme were adopted there would only be an additional need for a national organization and register of 'accredited independent practitioners' with its own accreditation scheme, codes of ethics and practice and a complaints' procedure. It would be essential for it to become a statutory or chartered organization, to ensure that no one could be a counsellor in independent practice without registration. The existence of two bodies would create considerable duplication of work that could be prevented by a National Register of Counsellors having two tiers of membership, the higher level being essential for an independent practitioner. This is a common situation in a number of chartered bodies. The Institution of Electrical Engineers, for example, has 'Associates' (not yet chartered, but training with an approved and Institution-monitored course, completion of which leads to chartered status), 'Members' who are chartered, and a more senior grade, 'Fellows', reserved for those who have achieved positions commanding the respect of the profession. While these measures are being debated and hopefully implemented, BAC could create either a new division or a new tier of membership for 'accredited independent practitioners'. This would in any case be advantageous, being similar to the situation that already exists for physiotherapists in private practice. All physiotherapists have to be chartered, but those in private practice can also belong to the Organisation for Chartered Physiotherapists in Private Practice. They pay an annual membership fee and in return receive regular information and newsletters. Some members also advertise *en bloc* to reduce costs. Counsellors in independent practice could benefit from such an organization; it would keep them in touch with one another, and newsletters, with relevant articles, would create an informal means for counsellors to monitor their work.

Once a single voluntary National Register has been formed there are three possibilities. The activity of counselling could be restricted by legislation to members of a regulated profession; the register could become government recognized, or it could be given legislative backing with the use of the title 'counsellor' being restricted. The first is relatively rare in Britain. Two professions which are regulated are pharmacists and architects. At present to call oneself an architect necessitates being on a register. However, a recent government sponsored report has recommended the deregulation of architects. An example of a profession with a government recognized national register is physiotherapy. The most likely way to restrict the use of 'counsellor' to specific people is via the statutory recognition of a charter. This involves applying to the Privy Council for a charter. In the short-term a government recognized National Register with self-regulation is likely, but perhaps in the long-term counselling will be a chartered profession. One advantage of a chartered body is that within their statutes they can build in the ability to swiftly discipline their members, a process which tends to be much longer when it has to go through the national legal system. A profession which is self-regulated also tends to act more jealously to safeguard its standards than other systems, since the ultimate sanction is to lose its charter and its public credibility.

It was mentioned in Chapter 4 that the lack of a fee structure undermines the full-time professional counsellor. Some chartered bodies, for instance the Royal Institute of British Architects, recommend fees for specific pieces of work, leaving it to the conscience of its members to decide whether they abide by this. Inevitably some practitioners will undercut others. The fees of private medical practitioners are partly regulated by the insurance companies which frequently pay for the treatment. They set rates for specified procedures. Some practitioners charge more than the set fee, only accepting patients who will pay the difference between the amount the insurance company will pay and their fee. It seems likely then that counselling will continue to have a wide range of fees and perhaps recommendations from the professional body for different types of work. At present BAC does give clients guidance on the likely range of fees (Information Sheet 5).

MONITORING AND EVALUATION

Monitoring and evaluation of counselling work are both essential, and particularly so while counselling is only self-regulated. At present with no voluntary or compulsory National Register, the undertaking of both these activities depends on the attitude of individual counsellors. It is a clear responsibility of all counsellors to monitor their work. Only in this way can the general public be safeguarded. It is worth repeating that clients of independent practitioners are particularly vulnerable to malpractice.

There are a number of ways of monitoring practice. The first is to seek accreditation. To do this counsellors have to review their own work and then submit it for peer review. Figures from the BAC accreditation scheme show that about 56 per cent of applicants for accreditation between March 1991 and January 1992 were successful (Lambers 1992), which suggests that the process has rigour and does discriminate. Once accreditation is achieved it is not for life, unlike most chartered bodies where it is assumed that chartered members accept responsibility for their continuing professional development (Grant 1992). BAC accredited counsellors have to re-accredit every five years. This may seem anomalous. However, as long as counselling is only self-regulated it does ensure that counsellors do continue to monitor their work, if only every five years.

Regular supervision also provides a forum in which counsellors can and should monitor their work. Apart from the usual functions of supervision, one of which is to review a counsellor's client load regularly, there are some important questions that an independent practitioner needs to be asked; such as:

Is the counsellor's assessment that a client needs long-term counselling appropriate?
Is the counsellor inducing inappropriate or unnecessary dependence?
Is the counsellor preventing termination?

These questions are all directed towards checking that a counsellor is neither deliberately nor in error keeping clients too long. Even if a client is prepared to pay, this is no reason to keep them in counselling longer than necessary.

Apart from external supervision which is at regular intervals, counsellors need to monitor their work from day to day. This internal supervision (Casement 1985: 30–56) consists of internal reflection, unfocused listening, and trial identification with the client. All these take place during a session, but it is useful to spend a few moments after a session to remember, and possibly write down, any words or phrases that stay in one's mind, or particularly vivid images or ideas that are difficult to shake off. A brief reflection on these will often help a counsellor recognize something that was not properly attended to or missed during the session.

It is even more important that counsellors evaluate their work to ascertain if their clients are satisfied and the outcome of the counselling was satisfactory. For a counsellor in independent practice, client satisfaction can on occasion be very directly evaluated. An important initial routine question to potential clients is how they came to the counsellor (see Chapter 4). If the answer is via a former client this indicates a satisfied earlier client. Obviously, as more former clients recommend a counsellor, the greater the validation of that counsellor's work. On occasion an ex-client's recommendation can reflect unresolved transference rather than satisfaction. In this instance the ex-client might punish a counsellor with an extremely difficult client or conversely reward with a 'present' of a client.

A more rigorous way of evaluating client satisfaction is the routine use of a brief questionnaire. Some EAPs use these at the completion of counselling. It is returned to the client's employer and is designed to check that the client was treated professionally throughout. The questions asked relate to the promptness of reply, the confidential handling of client's problems, and satisfaction with the outcome. All these questions are pertinent to any independent practitioner and the first two can be effectively evaluated by this method. Outcome is better evaluated at a later stage, some time after counselling has finished, in order to measure sustained change. How much later this should take place is a subject of ongoing debate. It needs to be long enough to provide a reasonable gap but not so long that the client may have lost interest in replying. Additionally, counsellors need feedback sooner rather than later in order to review their methods of working. A reasonable compromise might be three months after counselling has ended.

Other questionnaires assess such aspects as the client's mood, levels of anxiety, and ability to socialize. These need completing before counselling starts and also at a standard time after it has ended to assess what sustained changes have been made during this period. Questionnaires can also be used to check skills, for instance the ability to establish a therapeutic alliance. An example of this is the Horvath and Greenberg (1989) 'Development and Validation of the Working Alliance Inventory'. It is administered at the end of the third session and is completed independently by the counsellor and client. Correlation between the counsellor's and the client's perception of the process then indicates the effectiveness of the therapeutic alliance. If the correlation is low, this indicates that the counsellor needs to review his or her practice.

Although laborious, it is important periodically to review a session. Audio- or video-tapes are useful provided this has been agreed with the client in the initial contract and confidentiality rules are maintained. Analysis of such tapes is an important source of learning and can be used in supervision sessions. Listening to the tapes, counsellors recall what they experienced at particular moments and can often make sense of what looked like a *faux pas* (Kagan and Kagan 1991). It is also rewarding to find the good moments. We all need positive feedback at times!

Continuing professional development is closely allied to continued evaluation. The former is always a responsibility of any chartered practitioner regardless of profession. Undertaking courses, workshops and conferences and reading journals can all be used by counsellors to evaluate their current practice and compare it with others. Some journal articles use a considerable amount of client material and vignettes, for instance the *British Journal of Psychotherapy*, and these can be particularly illuminating. Others such as *Counselling* and *Counselling News* have articles on a wide range of topics of interest to counsellors. Another group of journals focuses on research: these are the *British Journal of Guidance and Counselling*, the *Journal of Counseling Psychology* and *Psychotherapy Research* (published by the Society for Psychotherapy Research). Much recent research has analysed audio- or video-tapes of sessions to identify 'therapist operations' immediately prior to client change (Hill and O'Grady 1985), sudden client insight (Elliott 1983), and 'good moments' (Mahrer et al. 1992). Therapist operations after clients have been dominant or controlling have also been studied (Lichtenberg and Barké 1981). Research of this type has an immediate use for counsellors, enabling them to consider what interventions to make and when.

All these methods of monitoring and evaluating are relevant whether a compulsory National Register is created or not. The question is, once a Register exists, can good practice then be assumed? In fact, no Register can prevent bad practice nor exclude the dishonest, but it does demonstrate and encourage good practice and discipline those who break the professional codes. If counselling is registered or chartered there will be a high percentage of practitioners in independent practice. This has implications of its own, as the protection offered to the general public by a National Register or Charter might be insufficient. One solution might be a system of statutory inspection of the service offered by counsellors. An inspector would have a statutory right to inspect the premises, to ensure that records are securely stored and to use a range of criteria to establish good practice. Relevant information might be a supervisor's report, samples of completed questionnaires (with the client's anonymity ensured) and yearly statistics. An alternative method of assessing might be for the chartered society to require all members and their clients to complete and return brief standard questionnaires to the society at the termination of counselling. These questionnaires would be different but might assess satisfaction and outcome. The results could be computerized and then comparisons made between the two perceptions of the same process. In time, the information would accumulate to indicate what actually is normal practice. This is unknown at the moment and there has been no research into what constitutes good or even normal practice. The chartered society's statutes could make it a disciplinary offence for a counsellor not to comply. Obviously this cannot be enforced upon clients, but over a period of time there would be data on the expected level of response from clients. If the level for a counsellor was very different from the norm, this would need explanation.

FUTURE DEVELOPMENTS

It is clear that the future must bring first a voluntary and then a government recognized National Register if clients are to be protected and counsellors respected. Even before this happens, there is much that counsellors in independent, private practice can do to show they are professional and can be trusted. Every opportunity should be taken to talk about counselling in general and the particular safeguards the responsible independent practitioner puts in place. Trust has to be built up and accurate information disseminated. It is also important to lobby politicians to persuade them of the need to ensure that government recognition of a Register of Counsellors happens soon and that in time statutory recognition of a charter is granted.

While the number of independent practitioners is likely to continue to grow, particularly in areas of the country where existing provision of counsellors is minimal, there is evidence that in London there is beginning to be an over-supply of counsellors. This may partly reflect that many inadequately trained people are setting up inappropriately and in this case registration will gradually filter these out and ultimately reduce the number of unregulated courses.

It has been mentioned that many independent practitioners also run courses as a way of varying their work and increasing their income, and sometimes to allow them to offer concessionary places to low-income clients. Registration, while rationalizing the courses that teach counselling skills and counselling, will not have any jurisdiction over the innumerable short courses on topics such as stress management, bereavement, and assertiveness training. A recent advertisement in a local paper offered to teach stress management, for a considerable fee. After nine hours of course work, two days' client observation and some home study, taking six weeks in all, trainees are led to expect earnings of £300–600 per week for 10–20 hours of work. Compulsory validation of courses is essential to protect the naïve and unwary from such unscrupulous operators.

There are many reasons for the boom in counselling in all the different contexts in which it is practised. For independent, private practitioners there is always concern about how to take counselling to the underprivileged, but perhaps it is more important to take part in schemes to educate society at large on how to meet the emotional needs of small children. They are our investment in the future and anything that improves the emotional health of people in general has a spin-off for society. This might ultimately reduce the demand for counselling as the 'peace dividend' has for armaments. Would that it could be so.

This does not mean that I am predicting, or wanting, the demise of counselling. I hope that counselling will be more freely available to people, regardless of means. Better emotional health will mean less long-term counselling work and more short-term work, with people seeking the help of a counsellor because they know it is inappropriate to burden friends and family at certain times. This change alone will result in a more rapid turnover and shorten waiting-lists. In a free market economy, counselling in the independent sector should be an option. I look to the day when it is properly regulated and there are sufficient competent chartered counsellors in all sectors and sufficient numbers in all areas of the country. Then the choice of counselling from a independent practitioner will be a positive one, not made on the basis of Hobson's choice. I would like to be part of such a profession.

Appendix A: Example of a pre-counselling leaflet

MARY BROWN

Accredited Counsellor

Short-term and long-term counselling for individuals

WHAT IS COUNSELLING?

Counselling offers you a place to explore difficulties you are having in your personal life with someone who is trained neither to judge nor advise you, but to explore and unlock your feelings, which may have been hidden for years. Past and present relationships will be talked about as well as your relationship with the counsellor. It may well be upsetting but it will help you to understand more about yourself. From this you may begin to feel less confused, or make changes in your life, or come to terms with things that can't be changed.

WHO IS IT FOR?

There are many reasons for seeking counselling. You may be feeling upset and distressed and have problems with your feelings, thoughts, relationships with others, or behaviour. You may have had a sudden life-crisis such as a bereavement, or have lost your job, or have been burgled. You may feel you lack direction and that life makes no sense.

HOW CAN YOU MAKE CONTACT?

You can either telephone or write. If you telephone you are likely to get my answerphone. Please leave a message and I will ring you back as soon as I can. You will be offered an initial meeting with me of one and a half hours to find out more about each other, and explore how best to approach your difficulties. By the end of this assessment, which might take two visits, you will be able to decide whether counselling is the right step for you and whether we can and want to work together. You may decide there and then, or go away and think about it.

WHAT ARE MY WORKING HOURS?

I usually work on Monday, Tuesday, Thursday and Friday from 08.30 to 18.00. On Wednesday I work from 18.00 to 20.00. I take six weeks holiday per year, including two weeks each at Christmas and Easter. I will give as much notice as possible of the timing of the other breaks.

WHAT DOES IT COST?

My fees are £X per hour and are reviewed in March each year. Sessions are usually regularly once a week. I charge for all contracted sessions which you decide not to keep. If I have to cancel a session I will, whenever possible, offer you an alternative appointment. If we cannot find a mutually convenient time I will not charge a fee for that missed session.

CODE OF ETHICS AND PRACTICE

I am a member of the British Association for Counsellors (BAC), who have a Code of Ethics and Practice for Counsellors. Copies are available on request. If I break these codes, you have the right and duty to make a formal complaint to BAC.

WHO AM I?

Before training as a counsellor, I was a volunteer counsellor with Cruse. I completed the two year part-time course at

Barchester College of Further and Higher Education (1976–78).
I have worked full-time as a counsellor for seven years. I am an
accredited counsellor (BAC 1988). I have had personal one-to-
one counselling for four years. I still have personal counselling
available to me should a personal problem or crisis occur. My
counselling work is supervised fortnightly.

WHERE DO I WORK?

I work from home in a part of my house solely kept for counselling. I enclose a map of how to find me. If coming by bus, a
number X comes from the centre of Barchester to the end of
Abbey Street. Ask for St Matthew's Church.

OTHER SERVICES

I am also an accredited supervisor and trainer (BAC). I therefore
supervise counsellors and run workshops and short training
courses (details on request). I am particularly interested in loss
and bereavement, and training people to develop their counselling skills.

You might stick a map here when sending the
leaflet to a potential client.
It might not be sensible to have a map on a leaflet
freely available to the
general public.

MARY BROWN SRN
26 Abbey St, Barchester
Tel:

Appendix B: Example of a letter confirming an appointment

MARY BROWN
Accredited Counsellor
26 Abbey Street
Barchester
Tel:

Dear

I am writing to confirm your appointment for an assessment session on   at   . We will need about an hour and a half to decide together whether you have come to the right place, and whether we can work together. If you arrive late I will not be able to carry on longer than this. I enclose a copy of my pre-counselling leaflet which confirms and adds to what I said on the phone. I hope this will answer some of your questions so you know what to expect.

I know you will want to be sure that our meetings are private and confidential, as do my other clients; to ensure this, and because I do not have a waiting-room, would you please arrive no more than ten minutes before the time of your appointment? If you are coming by car, again privacy is important. Please do not park outside my premises until ten minutes before your appointment time. Thank you.

Should you decide not to keep your appointment, would you please let me know at least 48 hours beforehand.

I look forward to meeting you.
Yours sincerely,

Appendix C: Example of a contract between counsellor and client

MARY BROWN
Accredited Counsellor

We are both making a commitment of time and energy to each other in deciding to work together. It is important for you to know what agreements we are making and so what to expect.

FREQUENCY OF SESSIONS

Sessions will be for one hour and will normally be at the same time and on the same day each week. This whole hour 'belongs' to you, whether you choose to attend or not. If you come five minutes from the end of 'our' time, I will be there. I will not offer your time to anyone else, even if you are away on holiday.

FEES

My fees are £X per hour and will be reviewed in March each year. I will give you a month's notice if I decide to raise them.

When you buy counselling you are giving yourself something of value. The fee is a statement about your importance to yourself, as well as being the source of my livelihood; therefore all sessions are paid for, whether you attend or not.

LETTERS AND TELEPHONE

There may be occasions when you feel the need to 'talk' to me between sessions, either by telephone or letter. It is rare that I can respond rapidly to you, so you may feel very rejected when I am slow to reply. Try first to work through the difficulty and then talk about it at the next session. There may be emergencies when you just cannot do this. As soon as I am free I will give you a maximum of 20 minutes on the phone. I will charge you for the counselling time on a pro rata basis. I know that when you make such a call it will be an emergency, and I trust that you will try to make the call at a time which respects my need for free time.

Letters are a useful way of containing your feelings and thoughts until the next session. If you post the letter to me it is unlikely that I will reply, but I will explore the contents of the letter at our next session together.

HOLIDAYS

I take six weeks holiday per year, two weeks each at Easter and Christmas and two weeks in the summer. I will give you as much notice as possible of my other breaks. I do not charge fees for missed sessions while I am on holiday.

CANCELLATION

There will be occasions when I shall not be able to give you your session because of illness, or because I am attending the occasional training session or meeting. I will give you as much notice as possible and, if I can, offer you alternative times. If you cannot come at any of the times I suggest, I will not charge you for the session that week.

CONFIDENTIALITY AND NOTES

The content of sessions are confidential to you and me. I will need to discuss our work with my supervisor but I will not

reveal your name. It is important that you also respect the confidentiality of our sessions. Although friends may be interested
and well-meaning, their comments are bound to affect our
relationship.

If you turn to your doctor because of your emotional difficulties,
it is important that he or she knows about me and vice versa,
and we both have your permission to confer, if necessary. I will
not communicate with your doctor without your permission
and knowledge of what I wish to discuss.

I do make brief notes after a session. These are securely stored
and there is no way you can be identified from the notes.

On occasions I would like to make audio-tapes. I will not do
this unless I have asked you before a session starts. I use these
tapes, which are securely stored and wiped after use, to monitor
my work.

TERMINATION

There may be times in the counselling when you feel very distressed and believe the counselling is not helping you. It is wise
to come and talk about these difficulties and not to suddenly
end the counselling. The reason for this is that many of us have
already experienced difficult and sudden losses. If this happens
in counselling as well, these losses have no chance to be understood and resolved.

If you hurt me or damage my property I will consider whether
I need to terminate counselling.

Normally you will know when you are ready to finish counselling and together we will work out the way that suits you.

PLEASE read this carefully, and check that this is what we agreed
together today. If there are any questions, ask me at the start of
our next session. These are our ground rules, unless you have
any queries.

Appendix D: Insurance companies specializing in policies for counsellors

Bartlett & Co. Ltd, Broadway Hall, Horsforth, Leeds LS18 4RS. Tel: (0532) 585711. Only available to members of BAC and BPS.

Devitt Insurance Services Ltd, Central House, 32–66 High Street, Stratford, London E15 2PF. Tel: (081) 519 0202.

Psychologists' Protection Society, Standalane House, Kincardine, Alloa, Clacks, FK10 4NX. Tel: (0259) 30785.

Appendix E: A sample page from an account book

YEAR ENDING APRIL 5 1995

Income

DATE	INCOME DESCRIPTION	£	p
2-5-94	167/22	100	00
2-5-94	168/08	100	00
2-5-94	169/21	75	00
2-5-94	Barchester Health Authority Fee } Travel Expenses } 170/17	250	00
2-5-94		15	00
5-5-94	172/20	25	00
5-5-94	Barchester F.E. College Supervision	45	00
3-5-94	171/07	25	00
3-5-94	172/20	25	00
3-5-94	178/19	25	00
3-5-94	174/24	45	00
	Brought forward p. 3	730	00
		2728	90
		3458	90

Expenditure

DATE	EXPENDITURE DESCRIPTION	NO.	£	p	SUPERVISION	POSTAGE	TELEPHONE	STATIONERY BOOKS PHOTO-COPYING	CONFERENCES & TRAINING COSTS	ADVERTISING	SECRETARIAL	PENSION INSURANCE ETC	TRAVEL & SUBSISTENCE	REPAIRS & SUNDRIES
2-5-94	Supervision	15	45	00	45 00									
2-5-94	Paper handkerchiefs	16	—	87										— 87
2-5-94	Barchester Health Authority Travel Expenses		15	00									15 00	
3-5-94	Postage	17	1	50		1 50								
3-5-94	Secretarial work	18	40	00							40 00			
5-5-94	Fees for training day	19	50	00					50 00					
5-5-94	Lunch	20	2	50									2 50	
10-5-94	Stationery	21	4	22				4 22						
13-5-94	Telephone bill	23	72	46			72 46							
	Brought forward p. 4		231	55	45 00	1 50	72 46	4 22	50 00	45 00	40 00	345 15	17 50	— 87
			685	72	45 00	10 64	—	12 99	—	45 00	120 00	345 15	87 00	19 94
			917	27	90 00	12 14	72 46	17 21	50 00		160 00		104 00	20 81

Appendix F: Useful BAC publications

Counselling and Psychotherapy Resources Directory – 5th edition
Training in Counselling and Psychotherapy – 8th edition
Recognition of Counsellor Training Courses
Careers in Counselling
Guide to Training Courses in the UK
Codes of Ethics and Practice:
   for Counsellors
   for Counselling Skills
   for Trainers
   for the Supervision of Counsellors

Information Sheets
Number 1 Confidentiality and the Law
Number 2 Counselling and Befriending
Number 5 Finding a Counsellor
Number 6 Counselling in Private Practice
Number 7 Careers and Training in Counselling
Number 8 Supervision
Number 9 Guidelines for the Employment of Counsellors
Number 10 What is Counselling?
Number 13 Evaluation and Counselling

Available from: 1 Regent Place, Rugby CV21 2PJ.
Tel: (0788) 550899.

References

Anderson, M. (1992) 'The need of the patient to be emotionally known: the search to understand a counter-transference dilemma', *British Journal of Psychotherapy*, 8, 247–52.

Bell, E. (forthcoming) *Counselling in HE and FE*. Buckingham: Open University Press.

Bond, T. (forthcoming) *Standards and Ethics for Counselling in Action*. London: Sage.

Brown, D. and Pedder, J. (1979) *Introduction to Psychotherapy*. London: Tavistock Publications.

Casement, P. (1985) *On Learning from the Patient*. London: Tavistock Publications.

Dyne, D. (1988) 'Whither "Rugby"? – towards a profession of psychotherapy', *British Journal of Psychotherapy*, 4, 148–55.

East, P. (forthcoming) *Counselling in Medical Settings*. Buckingham: Open University Press.

Einzig, H. (1989) *Counselling and Psychotherapy: Is It for Me?* Rugby: British Association for Counselling.

Elliott, R. (1983) '"That in your hands": a comprehensive process analysis of a significant event in psychotherapy', *Psychiatry*, 46, 113–29.

Feltham, C. (1992) 'The stress of being a counsellor: a personal view', *Counselling News*, 7, 4–5.

Ferenczi, S. (1928) 'The elasticity of psycho-analytic technique', in *Final Contributions to the Problems and Methods of Psycho-analysis*. London: Hogarth (1955).

Foster, J. (1971) *The Foster Report on Scientology*. London: HMSO.

Freud, S. (1913) 'On beginning the treatment', in *The Case of Schreber; Papers on Technique and Other Works*. Standard Edition, 12. London: Hogarth (1958).

Freud, S. (1926) *The Question of Lay Analysis*. Penguin Freud Library, Volume 15. Harmondsworth: Penguin.

Freud, S. (1927) *Postscript to 'The Question of Lay Analysis'*. Penguin Freud Library, Volume 15. Harmondsworth: Penguin.

Grant, J. (1992) 'BAC accreditation – what value?', *Counselling*, 3, 89.

Halmos, P. (1978) *The Faith of the Counsellors*. London: Constable.

Hawkins, P. and Shohet, R. (1989) *Supervision in the Helping Profession*. Milton Keynes: Open University Press.

Hay, L. (1988) *You Can Heal Your Life*. London: Eden Grove Editions.

Hill, C. E. and O'Grady, K. E. (1985) 'List of therapist intentions illustrated in a case study with therapists of varying theoretical orientations, *Journal of Counseling Psychology*, 32, 3–22.

Horvath, A. O. and Greenberg, L. S. (1989) 'Development and validation of the working alliance inventory', *Journal of Counseling Psychology*, 36, 225–33.

Jones, E. (1964) *The Life and Works of Sigmund Freud*. Harmondsworth: Penguin (abridged edition of three volumes published by Hogarth).

Kagan, N. I. and Kagan, H. (1991) 'IPR – A Research/Training Model', in Dowrick and Associates (eds), *Practical Guide to Using Video in the Behavioural Sciences*. Canada: Wiley.

King's Fund (1991) *Counselling for Regulated Infertility Treatments*. London: King's Fund Centre.

Kopp, S. (1977) *Back to One*. Palo Alto: Science and Behavior Books, Inc.

Lambers, E. (1992) 'Counselling accreditation', *Counselling*, 3, 81–2.

Lee, C. and Six, T. L. (1992) 'Counsellor licensure: the American experience', *Counselling*, 3, 93–5.

Lichtenberg, J. W. and Barké, K. H. (1981) 'Investigation of transactional communication relationship patterns in counseling', *Journal of Counseling Psychology*, 28, 471–80.

Lyall, D. (forthcoming) *Counselling in the Church*. Buckingham: Open University Press.

Mahrer, A. R., White, M. V., Howard, M. T. *et al.* (1992) 'How to bring about some good moments in psychotherapy sessions', *Psychotherapy Research*, 2, 252–65.

Oram, J. E. D. (1987) *Psychotherapy – Is It for You?* Private Publication.

Palmer, I. (1993) 'The counselling and psychotherapy resources directory (CPRD). Results of a survey', *Counselling*, 4, 3–4.

Pilgrim, D. (1992) 'Principle or prejudice?', *Counselling News*, 8, 9.

Rowan, J. (1992) 'Principle or Prejudice?', *Counselling News*, 8, 8.

Storr, A. (1979) *The Art of Psychotherapy*. London: Secker & Warburg and William Heinemann Medical Books.

Szasz, T. (1965) *The Ethics of Psycho-analysis*. New York: Basic Books.

Temperley, J. (1984) 'Settings for psychotherapy', *British Journal of Psychotherapy*, 1, 101–12.

Thorne, B. (1992) *Carl Rogers*. London: Sage.

Trayner, B. and Clarkson, P. (1992) 'What happens if a psychotherapist dies?', *Counselling*, 3, 23–24.

Tyndall, N. (1993) *Counselling in the Voluntary Sector*. Buckingham: Open University Press.
Wallis, J. H. (1973) *Personal Counselling*. London: George Allen & Unwin.
Winnicott, D. W. (1972) *The Maturational Processes and the Facilitating Environment*. London: Hogarth.

Index